G000165866

MIND AND MOVEMENT

The Practice of Coex

By the same Author

Mystic Man
Yoga & Relaxation
Do You Dream?
Yoga & Childbirth
Yield
The Instant Dream Book

MIND AND MOVEMENT

The Practice of Coex

Tony Crisp

The C.W. Daniel Company Limited,
1, Church Path,
Saffron Walden,
Essex. CB10 1JP.

First published in Great Britain in 1987
by The C.W. Daniel Company Limited
1 Church Path, Saffron Walden
Essex, England

© Tony Crisp 1987

ISBN 0 85207 182 5

Designed by Tina Dutton
Production in association with
Book Production Consultants, Cambridge
Typeset by Best-set Typesetter Ltd.
Printed and bound by Billings, Worcester

Contents

INTRODUCTION   1

CHAPTER ONE...COEX – WHAT IT IS   7

The creative and healing human potential –
What it is and how it works – Cooperation with
the self-regulatory process – Its connection with
muscular tension and the dream process –
Extending awareness.

CHAPTER TWO...HONOURING   28
YOURSELF – THE PRACTICE OF COEX

Examples from everyday life – Sex emotion and
holding back – Hunches and the Feeling Sense –
Creative Imagination and the Seed meditation –
Working with the unconscious – The power of a
partner – Creative listening – The Seed Group.

CHAPTER THREE...OPENING THE   53
DOORS OF MIND AND BODY

Touching life in us – Danced from within –
Movements to free life process – Movement and
meditation – Loosening oneself through sounds
– Levels of awareness – The urge to health – Fear
as a block to health – Is it a cure-all?

CHAPER FOUR...CREATIVE AND   80
HEALING FACETS OF COEX

Dealing with specific questions and problems –
How to focus on inner resources – Signals from
within – Healing the body – Traumas of
childbirth – Working through old hurts.

CHAPTER FIVE...THE DREAM AND COEX 102

The blind spot in regard to dreams – Dreams
and self-regulation – Entering a dream while
awake – Knowing your dream through posture
and body movement – Do you like eating
people? – Dina Glouberman's Creative
Visualization – Learning to trust oneself.

CHAPTER SIX...TEACHING COEX 111

Teaching body skills – Detailed relaxation
techniques – Instructions for group leaders –
Finding unconscious tensions – Posture work –
Relaxed movement – Daring to be free – The
fear of being oneself – Postures and feelings –
How to enter the 'mind' through the body –
Coming out of withdrawal – Feeling Low/
Feeling High – The Earth the Seed and the Sun –
Awareness transforms – Standing and walking
anew.

CHAPTER SEVEN...INDIVIDUAL AND SOCIAL IMPLICATIONS 129

New views of death and life – The temptation to
'go Eastern' in the unconscious – Transcendence
or war – The voice of ones own experience –
Sam and fear on the streets – Sex and
manipulation – Life before birth – Life is a love
affair – Who are you? – Escalation of
responsibility.

CHAPTER EIGHT...SELF REGULATION 148

Homeostasis – The Wisdom of the Body –
Self-regulation growth and the mind – Hypnosis
and false neurosis – Reich and The Emotional
Plague – Self-regulation and its place in our life.

How humans in different cultures have used
their inner resources of self-regulation – Coex in
New Guinea – Shaktipat, the Indian way to
enlightenment – Hallucination or inner
knowlege? – Trances, Spirit healing and
possession – Buddhism and the way of
liberation – Zen, Tibetan Secret teachings and
Vipassana – Christianity's unwanted secret –
Saint Paul, killer of the inner life – Mesmer,
father of modern psychotherapy – Carl Jung
linking East and West – Aurobindo and integral
yoga – Reich and the cosmic energy – From
Guru to self responsibility – Subud, God's
chosen people – Burying old dogmas – Dianetics
and co-counselling – Ronnie Laing daring to
care – The Japanese have Seitai – Love is the key.

Introduction

It is new years eve of 1986 as I write this introduction. The book beyond these pages has already been written. Over the past few weeks I have received cards and letters from people who have used the techniques and approaches described in it. In wondering how best to tell you about what this book contains, and what it may have to offer, I cannot think of any better way than allowing these letters to tell their own story.

The most exuberant letter was sent by Paul, a well known musician. The SEED GROUP he mentions is one of the approaches to personal healing and creativity described fully in chapter six. Paul writes:

> I thank you again for the Seed Group experience at Atsitsa. With that I let go of so much accumulated rubbish! When I got back I had a session of Soul Directed Therapy and haven't looked back. Those two experiences must rank among the most important of my life. In fact my life is rolling, my creativity is rolling, my relationships are rolling!! I hope you are too!

Here are two short letters, the first from Sarah who says:

> Life has been somewhat difficult and confusing lately – not such a bad thing, but I can't see when it's going to sort itself out. I'm still with Michael but also seeing Steve. I just don't know what I want. Still, here's to 1986 and hopefully some decision making!
>
> Michael has been doing coex here in D . . .–amazingly – which has been very useful, thanks to you.

From a very different situation Tony writes:

Just a line of thanks for your having passed on to me the practice of coex. It is a path which has deepened and broadened over the years and although it functions differently it is still a source of eternal life. All my love, Tony.

The last letter is much longer, but from it a fuller idea of what coex is, and how it works in ones life can be gained. It is from Pat Hudson who studied with me a few years ago. Since then she has explored in many different directions and has brought coex into her life and love in an everyday sense. She writes:

I want to write to you about a dream and its process which I had a couple of nights ago. It's a marvellous dream. But first I need to say that there seems to be a tremendous healing process taking place in my inner being in three different areas. **1.** I have been experiencing a growing sense of forgiveness love and compassion towards my mother. I see her as a very vulnerable, sensitive spirit crippling herself by alcoholism and arthritis because she didn't and doesn't know how to deal with what society puts on her. **2.** I am becoming so much more alive sexually with my husband. It really astounds me at my age – fifty next birthday. I feel so much more loving and understanding towards him too. I am much more ready to receive his full-cream – milk kind of love. **3.** He and I have been going to Blackpool once every fortnight to visit a recently bereaved aunt of his and this experience is turning out to be so healing for me. In the past I have hated **common Blackpool** and its **common** people. Now I have turned right round to find that I actually love the whole Blackpool experience, common-ness and all. Instead of feeling separate and superior – I really thought I was once – I feel so linked with those people. I love being in the crowds on the sea front. I love them wearing their purple tinsel wigs and foam plastic hats. Thank God I'm losing that awful sense of superiority. Goodbye – I'm well rid of you.
Now for the dream. First of all it pushed me into reluctant wakefulness from a deep sleep in the middle of the night. I tried to kid myself that I would remember it next morning, but I was obliged to put on the light and

write it down. It was one of my sobbing, sobbing, sobbing dreams which I've had now and then over the years. I had been doing dream work with a friend during the day, and I had told her about a sobbing dream I had the previous week. I said I had never got to the bottom of why I had such dreams. In this dream I was sobbing down to my very guts. The scene was a man, his wife and a lodger. It was in Victorian times and the woman wore a long white dress. She loved her husband with all of herself. The three of them were sitting at a small round table, and the lodger had to expose the husband as a betrayer of her love. She was sobbing and felt as if everything was wiped away and made as nothing. It seemed to her the basis of her life was taken away.

Then the husband and she were walking along a river, she in a long white dress, still sobbing, knowing life would never be the same. And that was the end of the dream – yet it wasn't the end because more was to come. I lay half awake dreamily wondering how Garry my husband had betrayed me. He never has, I know that, so I was puzzled. I kept sniffing around wanting to go deeper when suddenly a vision swept through me. I was standing deep down inside myself on the edge of a black hole, a black precipice, and I was shouting, 'Well. what do you mean you silly devil?' It was as if I was shouting down to the me right at the **wellspring** of my being. I came more awake, had a laugh at the daftness of it, then suddenly realised the black hole was a birth canal. It wasn't my birth canal but my mother's. Then the whole thing began to flow. I suddenly knew with utter certainty that when I was in my mother's womb I was totally loved I can't tell you how marvellous it felt to know that love again – being totally, safely, securely lapped in love. I simply lay there experiencing the love. I knew, with a great sense of compassion, under-standing and forgiveness that as soon as I left the womb my mother couldn't love me the same way, couldn't cope with the stresses life put on her. I remembered a vision I had when I was with you in Devon. I saw my mother's breast dripping milk, a thin watery, vinegary milk and I burst into tears saying I wanted full-cream milk. I now felt totally linked with my mother again. All the rage and anger which had gradually been dropping away over the past few months was now gone. The tremendous linking remained.

After that lot I lay in bed awake feeling happy. I lay awake for about two hours. I realised I had never been able to accept love – never been able to accept Gary's full-cream-milk love. I was constitutionally unable to.

When I first met Pat she struck me as someone with very **frozen** feelings, especially in regard to her sexuality. It therefore gave me a lot of pleasure to hear her news of change. But I wondered what Pat had needed to be or do to find such satisfying transformation. I wrote to her telling her this. She replied:

The first thing which sprang to mind when I read your words **'someone as frozen as you were'** was a brief dream I had when I was first with you. I was standing in front of an enormous iceberg. In my hand was a little ice-pick and I was picking away at this great big berg. How vivid and wonderful. **I have never stopped picking away at that berg since.**

This **picking away** has taken many forms. I have for some time worked with three friends doing explorative counselling work each week. None of us are trained, and we use all sorts of tools such as Reichian and Gestalt work. Through this I have come across much that needed to be made aware in myself, and have had three big traumatic sessions. So big that each time I was ill and had to go to bed for two or three days to recover. During one such session feelings about my religious upbringing arose. As a teenager I longed and searched for the **living spirit**. I made the mistake of searching in the Church of England. The phrase comes, I searched for bread and you gave me a stone.' Kneel down. Stand up. Put your hands thus. Say this. Sing this. Nothing but stones. Such rage erupted from me I began vomiting green bile and kept on for almost two days.

So I continue coming across chunks of stuff like that. I see it as searching for the inner flame of myself. I am no longer living a false self as I did **for at least eighteen years of my life**. I see that false self as socially imposed

– but I accepted it. It was when the pain of living by this false self grew too great that I had to break out and came down to work with you. I have worked at stripping away the false bits and re-building the realer me ever since.

Coex is the way of working with the spontaneous process which led Pat to remember her mother's love in the womb. It is the function in us which produced the healing she found. It is the magical force which created Pat's dream, her visions, her gradual change. It is a process which has been so often overlooked, twisted into a mystery, covered with the ornate overlay of religious ritual and dogma. Yet it is something alive in each of us. It awaits our contact with it if we dare to look and meet the challenges of our own life and existence.

CHAPTER I

Coex – What it is

Carl Jung said that within each of us are resources of information and wisdom which are usually overlooked. He called this aspect of human experience the Transcendent Function. People who were able to work with this function, he said, experienced meaningful change from negative feelings and attitudes to more inclusive and positive ones. Often they found healing of physical ills too. Yet although Jung saw the Transcendent Function as a natural part of a persons resources – a spontaneous and self-regulatory source of healing – he never explained clearly to the public how they could use it themselves. His method has remained largely clinical and in the hands of professional 'Jungians'.

Others, like Dr Wilhelm Reich, have also described this source of healing, but still they have left a gap in their explanation. Namely they have not described in a way understandable to the public what the source of healing and help is, and how it can be tapped.

On the other hand many ancient cultures, in traditional teachings such as found in Yoga, Tai Chi and Meditation, have attempted to make publicly available knowledge of how to use this internal and wonderful process. Their symbolism and viewpoint is so different to ours however, that it is difficult to accept or understand many of their rather strange claims. This was made very plain to me while working in Japan with my wife Hyone. She had been helping a man, who was obviously very tense, to release the tension in his muscles. As this occurred he experienced powerful spontaneous movement, which is a feature of the self-regulatory process. Afterwards the man came to us with some of the other Japanese people attending the class and they asked us what point on the body or nervous system we had pressed to produce so powerful a response. They were so steeped in the oriental viewpoint expressed in acupuncture, they felt what they had experienced must have been produced from pressure points. To the Western structure of thought, much in acupuncture still remains outside of rational explanation. In my years of work in this field I have attempted both to understand in a Western sense what that Japanese man experienced, and to explain it in a way which makes it available for other ordinary people like myself to use.

During a period when I had just gone through divorce, the starting of a new relationship, and taking over a tumbledown property, I developed a permanent pain in my right forearm. I talked about this to a doctor who diagnosed it as tennis elbow. He told me there was nothing I could do except avoid exertion. As I was working to renovate our house, that was difficult, and the pain continued for six months without any change. I decided to ask my unconscious if there was anything I could do to help the condition. It was a technique I had used many times before, so had some experience of. Holding in mind the pain in the arm I waited for the responses to arise from within. Soon, spontaneous fantasies and ideas bubbled into awareness, almost as if someone were explaining the situation to me. I was led to understand that during the past year I had not only been working hard physically to renovate the building, but because of divorce, family conflict within my new relationship, plus the change of home, I had experienced much stress and anger. During my sawing, planing and hammering, I had discharged much of this anger and stress. As with any hard work, the cells in my right arm had broken down, but the anger and tension had prevented the cells from regenerating adequately.

As this insight emerged I could see what a shrewd summary of my recent unconscious attitudes it was. The emerging explanation went on to say that each cell is a tiny individual life, and in the body, they each take on a particular task. Some live as workers in the muscles; some are thinking beings in the brain, and some act as transformers, as in the liver. Each cell depends upon the others to cooperatively share food, oxygen and pleasure.

The cells in my arm didn't mind the hard work, but they needed to share the pleasures of eating, music and love making. I had been unconsciously deluging them with anger and tension, and denying them laughter and relaxation.

I started to use this information. For instance when I ate I would consciously allow the pleasure I felt in my mouth to be felt by the rest of my body, particularly the right arm. When I made love, I attempted to relax and let my whole body feel the pleasure, not keep it in the genitals. I frequently concentrated on my right arm, relaxing it and allowing pleasure felt elsewhere to flow to it. Within a week it was completely free of the pain, and the problem has never returned.

The technique of consciously cooperating with or listening to the processes of life active in the unconscious, and allowing them to become known, I call Coex. I have coined the word from two other words – consciousness and expansion – because the process of coex is partly that of expanding our awareness into areas of ourself previously unconscious. It holds in it many exciting possibilities, such as:-

1 Tapping the activity of natural forces in us toward healing of physical and psychological problems.
2 Gaining information which we hold within us, but which is usually unconscious.
3 Using the creative process of the unconscious to enrich our work and relationships.
4 Tuning into the body's self regulating processes to discover a spontaneous form of exercise or dance which releases tension and keeps the body fit.
5 Through expanded awareness discovering our connections with the rest of life and cosmos.

So what is coex, and what makes it function?

During 1968, while teaching relaxation techniques to people at the Tyringham Naturopathic Clinic in Buckinghamshire, I found the first clues to an exciting possibility in human beings. I had been teaching the usual form of relaxation in which one consciously tenses the muscles, then relaxes them. As an aid to people experiencing the pleasure of dropping tension as fully as possible, I often went to each person in the class and gently lifted an arm or leg. The aim was to give them the experience of someone else moving their body, so they could give up their own effort or tension. I found that many people's limbs were very difficult to move because they were rigid with tension. Surprisingly when I asked the person how they felt, they would usually say they felt relaxed and comfortable. Meeting this in person after person, no matter their age or sex, led me to realise how ineffective 'normal' forms of relaxation and stress release were. Also, more important, it showed that many of us are living with quite enormous unconscious tensions operating in us. Unconscious because the people I tested were unaware of their tenseness, and 'felt' relaxed. Yet to maintain the sort of muscular effort which makes an arm or leg difficult to move uses a great deal of energy. If you lived with such tensions, because of the energy wasted in maintaining them, you would have less energy to use in the other departments of your life.

I started to search for ways I could help people to release such tensions. Because people have always lived with tension and the forces of unconscious life within them, many men and women in the past and present have attempted to understand them. Each age and culture has developed its own approach, but they all have evident similarities. This is because they are dealing with the same inner activities. In general these different approaches break down into two different types. Historically the approach was usually of a very religious or sectarian nature. At the present the approach to the unconscious is often clinical, as in psychiatry. So in looking for already established techniques there was the choice of a clinical approach or that of a sect. Yet the forces of life in us are not bounded by authoritarian psychiatry nor by the narrow beliefs of a sect. Both of these groups attempt to own what belongs to everyone. So I sought to find what is common and functional in the different approaches.

For instance, as long ago as the seventeen hundreds Franz Mesmer found that by helping people to relax muscular tension, but remain open to movement, there was a spontaneous cathartic healing action. The person experienced spontaneous movements and feelings which led to the healing of their illness.

In this century, Dr. Wilhelm Reich, working from the background of a medical doctor, a biologist, and a Freudian psychoanalyst, did not feel content with the usual years of analysis needed to help people with serious psychological difficulties. From the standpoint of the body and mind being a unity, he began to look for signs of the mental condition in the state of the body. He found that all his patients had unconscious abdominal tension. One patient who was resisting change in his life exhibited powerful neck tensions. People repressing their emotions usually had tensions in their rib cage, whereas restrained sexuality produced tensions and pain in the pelvis and lower back. Many of our commonly used words, such as 'stiffnecked', 'held back', or 'stonehearted', are recognitions of how our attitudes shape our body tensions.

Reich observed that when any of these tensions were released a great deal of physical and/or emotional energy was also released. In fact the tension was a block or suppression of the natural flow of energy in our being. The energy itself can be expressed as physical movement, sexuality, emotions, drives such as parental caring, or the process of thinking. Usually, as a tension dissolves, the person experiences spontaneous movements. These are an extension to the usual spontaneous movements we make all the time, such as breathing, sneezing and yawning. But they are often movements we do not associate with general spontaneous activity.

Reich noticed, as had Mesmer before him, that if this spontaneous release of movement and feeling was allowed and worked with, the person was helped toward greater equilibrium. Reich also defined that the spontaneous movements occured through the release of tension. He saw such physical and emotional release as an expression of the homeostatic or self regulating process. Homeostasis is the function in our being which directs such activities as the balancing of body heat, and blood pressure, and is behind the regulation of growth. Jung and Hadfield also speak of dreams as being connected with this self regulatory function, acting in the area of the mind. They see dreams as helping to keep psychological balance, just as perspiration helps to keep a physical balance through loss of excess heat.

To clarify just what activities in human beings Reich and Mesmer were dealing with we need to look at some typical experiences of coex in action.

The first is that of a woman – Linda – who came to me at the recommendation of her doctor because she was 'on the verge of a breakdown'. Linda was married for the second time, had three children from her first marriage, and felt very tense. She was the first person I taught coex to in a one-to-one situation. Until then I had been teaching general relaxation, and as this hadn't helped Linda I asked if she wanted to learn coex as I thought it might be useful to her. She agreed and we decided to work once a week until we could see if she benefited or not. During the first session I began by asking Linda to stand while I moved her arms and body to see if there were any obvious muscular tensions. When I moved her arms by lifting them away from her hips, I found there was a point, when her hands were about a foot away from her body, where her arms remained suspended by shoulder tensions. I asked her to be aware of this without interfering. She did this as well as she could, and her arms remained suspended in the tension for about half an hour before we finished the session.

In the second session the tensions in the shoulders [deltoid] were found again and her arms remained suspended. The reason for this waiting is that prior to leaving the limbs in the position held by the tension, the person is usually unaware of having the tensions. If one 'relaxes the tension away' it does not in fact disappear, it merely slips back into the unconscious. By leaving it showing, so to speak, what was unconscious enters into awareness. The person is then in a learning situation. They learn to be aware of and allow into consciousness something that was unconscious. I see this as learning the skill to work with unconscious content. So once more I encouraged Linda to be aware of the tensions without interfering by relaxing them away or by trying to interpret what the tension meant. As she did this small jerks occurred in her arms. I assured her this was all right as she felt slightly disturbed by these spontaneous spasms. As it was a completely new experience, it took her a while to learn the ability to allow her body freedom of movement without interfering or stopping its activity. I therefore explained to her that the spasms were the muscular tension beginning to discharge, and that learning to allow the discharge was rather like learning to ride a bicycle − it was a new skill which becomes an easy habit through practice. We spent a full hour allowing these small spontaneous movements before finishing this second session.

This stage of honouring simple movement is important in coex because all the processes and expressions of life in us is expressed as the swing between movement and relaxation. Obvious movements in this connection are the heartbeat, breathing, and the peristaltic action of the digestive tract. The feeling reactions we experience as an organism in relationship to our environment can also be thought of as movements expressive of a life process. Consciousness is a 'life process', and when we cry or feel angry, our bodies make movements to express these feelings. Crying is a very strong muscular movement, and includes subtler but powerful movements such as the discharge of tears. Anger too involves a lot of physical movements, including faster heartbeat, glandular discharge, and maybe powerful punching or kicking. Sex expresses as strong and subtle body movements. If through tension or suppression we hold back what our being is feeling in response to our environment, we block these powerful and subtle motivations to MOVE. Therefore, in the body we can often find these blocked motivations as muscular tension. If we release the tension, then the self regulatory process in us begins to express the movements. And do not forget that here I am talking about movements as including glandular discharge, tears, emotions, muscular activity, and mental functioning.

Supposing what we are holding back are the movements connected with sexuality. Supposing we have done this because we have either a fear of it, or have been hurt in connection with it. In allowing a tension to become conscious which we had been unknowingly using to immobilise the pelvis, we would, in a sense, be uncovering a powerful 'NO'. i.e. "No, I will not allow sexuality and its accompanying movements because they are frightening or painful." By letting the tension remain in consciousness it usually begins to vacillate to a 'YES' – it begins to break down or release. For a while it may swing backwards and forwards between the 'yes' and 'no'. Physically this means the tension releases for a moment but snaps back again, causing jerks or trembling. Sometimes, if a great deal of energy is held back by the tension being released, the trembling will be intense and the person may feel cold. Occasionally the person then complains that the room is very cold.

Linda began to feel she was learning to cooperate with her inner process in the third session. She began to discover how to allow the tension to release without interfering. The jerks then became tentative movements. Her hands spontaneously moved to her lower abdomen and made pressing movements. At this point neither of us understood what this meant, or what her inner process was beginning to express. Because the movements were strong enough, and Linda could allow the spontaneous action easily now, I suggested she lay down instead of standing.

The fourth and final session began with Linda lying on a blanket. Her arms quickly began the spontaneous movements to her abdomen without needing any priming by finding the tensions. The movements were much stronger this time and her whole body became involved. Her knees drew up and her abdominal area domed. She made very little sound – some people are extremely vocal – but she was intensely absorbed in the movements for nearly an hour before they stopped and she lay peacefully. She then sat up and told me she had experienced something extraordinary. She said that four years earlier she had been divorced and went to live in Spain with her children. While there she had an affair with a Spaniard and became pregnant. Because she already had children and was not wanting to stay with the man, she had an abortion. During her body movements it had seemed to her as if the life in her had said the abortion had hurt it. It then led her through the spontaneous movement to complete the process of giving birth to that baby, and in that way she now felt whole. The process of birth which had been cut off had been able to complete itself.

Although I have already quoted the next experience in my publication *The Instant Dream Book*. I use it again here because it describes the spontaneity and unanticipated nature of coex so well. Su had attended a seminar at which I explained how to work with coex. She describes her experience as follows:

When Tony came to explain coex to the group, I had just reached the point of despair with my marriage. A few days before I had taken the first step towards breaking it. From the first my experience of coex wove itself, directly or indirectly, into my outer life. It was never a separate thing going on inside only.

Tony explained to us about letting whatever came, come. I did not understand too well, but lay down with the others and he came to each of us briefly and moved our arms, and left us lying. Perhaps two minutes had passed when I felt a distinct twitching around my brow, which was repeated, and then it spread down my face, a downward pressing movement. My face was involved then in a big muscular movement, pressing down, seeming to flatten the face, and then spread down the body towards the feet. Gradually my whole body became involved in big waves of pressing movement which flowed down, lifting and tossing my legs, so that my heels were banging on the floor. Wave succeeded wave. I did as he said, and let it happen, using the skills to relax which I had learnt. I wasn't afraid, although I couldn't imagine what was happening to me. Instead I felt happy and elated, warmed through. I knew I had found something of great significance, but it was many months before I could put words to it. It remained an intriguing mystery, like a dropping away of chains, or a touching of promise, while I passed through the pain of divorce. I feel that my experience that day released considerable energy. It did not break my marriage – that would have happened anyway. But I received strength which I used for my needs at that time. Months later it came to me with the force of revelation, that I had been born that day.

Linda and Su's experience demonstrate that simply by changing the way they related to themselves they opened the door to a power and expressive part of their nature. Neither of them previously suspected what was hidden behind a change of attitude. It is worth noting also that while Su's experience was an unusual form of movement, Linda's was a particular theme. But neither of them were haphazard or random. Noting this same fact generally in people using coex, I felt it must express some basic process and wondered what it was. Gradually I have come to believe that one of the main processes at work is that which also lies behind the creation of dreams.

All mammals are known to experience a stage of sleep characterized by rapid eye movements [REM] behind closed eyelids. In humans this REM sleep in connected with dreaming. Until recently however, it was not known just what animals dreamt. But while investigating a condition called 'narcolepsy', a condition characterized by sudden and uncontrollable lapses into REM sleep in animals, Adrian Morrison at the University of Pennsylvania, uncovered some interesting information. Usually, in animals and humans, a small area of the pons in the brain, prevents our muscular system from responding to signals from the brain while we are dreaming. Morrison noticed that in mammals in which this area is damaged, full body movements are made during REM sleep. This shows that not only can the dream process create a spontaneous fantasy or experience we call a dream; not only can it invest the dream with deeply felt emotions or creative ideas, it can also be expressed as full body movement. Except in cases of sleep walking, such body activities are prevented by the pons from being expressed except perhaps in small jerks or movements. Nevertheless, speech, walking, dancing, fighting and making love, are all frequent dream subjects. So human beings have at least two centres which can direct body processes. We are used to making conscious decisions about walking or moving our hands, but few of us suspect that another part of our being outside our conscious volition is capable and practised in making full body movements and expressing itself in complex speech.

I believe that by letting things happen without criticism or interference, we are actually allowing the dream process to break through into our waking life and express itself in full body movements, speech, a dramatic theme, and deeply felt emotions. This is another reason why I have named this process Consciousness Expansion, because the usual boundaries of our awareness have been enlarged. We begin to be aware of things that usually happen to our psyche only while we sleep. Our consciousness is expanded to the point where it includes a realm of experience which is in many ways different from our waking world. In quite a real sense we begin to 'wake up' in what was sleep. As exciting as that is, it might not have much point, apart from a novelty, if it were not for the many possibilities the awakening holds. Freud was reasonably cautious in ascribing to the dream function anything which was not easily observed, yet if we look at his definitions of what occurs in dreams, we begin to understand something of the possibilities in coex.

1 Dreams are 'thoughts-in-pictures'. It seems likely that early in human evolution, prior to the development of complex spoken language, people used images as tools of thought instead of words. So dreams may be in part a return to this earlier level of thinking. Silberer, a student of Freud's, gives an example in that while falling asleep he was thinking about something he had written, and decided to tidy up its rough edges. He then realised he was dreaming of planing a rough piece of wood.

2 Dreams are 'ego alien'. This means that they happen to us rather than that we deliberately create them. David Foulkes points out that this has led many people to believe that dreams are given to us by God or gods, or come from the dead, or from some force outside ourselves. In general, however, all this means is that they arise from a motivation in ourselves which lies outside our conscious volition and awareness.

3 Dreams are 'hallucinatory'. In dreams we create, seemingly outside of ourselves, apparently real characters in environments which we feel deeply involved in. When we sit and have a daydream or think, there is not this sense of really doing or being what we are thinking. Yet in a dream this is so.

4 Dreams are 'drama'. Most of our dreams are not merely

a tumbling kaleidoscope of images and feelings. They have definite plots, with a beginning middle and end. They describe scenes which are understandable to other people. Sometimes they are as well produced as a first class film or play. In fact, many stories have been written from dreams. Nothing so highly structured could be the result of random neuronal firing. Because of this, Freud thought dreams must be 'constructed by a highly complicated activity of the mind'.

5 Dreams have different 'moral standards'. In dreams we rape, pillage, murder and adventurously act in ways we would resist with horror in waking life.

6 Dreams have access to a more active 'association of ideas'. This means that not only can we have a much wider response to any idea we hold in mind, but also the response jumps beyond the usual pathways of our thoughts. It can thus be very creative.

Since Freud's research, many other people have added to his findings. So Jung, Hadfield, and people like Caldwell, writing about waking dreaming in therapeutic situations, have enlarged the understanding of dream functions. Therefore we can add to the above definitions as follows:-

7 Dreams are compensatory or 'self-regulatory'. Hadfield says of this:

There is in the psyche an automatic movement toward readjustment, toward an equilibrium, toward a restoration of the balance of our personality. This automatic adaptation of the organism is one of the main functions of the dream as indeed it is of bodily functions and of the personality as a whole. This idea need not cause us much concern for this automatic self-regulating process is a well known phenomenon in Physics and Physiology. The function of compensation which Jung has emphasised appears to be one of the means by which this automatic adaptation takes place, for the expression of repressed tendencies has the effect of getting rid of conflict in the personality. For the time being, it is true, the release may make the conflict more acute as the repressed emotions emerge, and we have violent dreams from which we wake with a start. But by this means, the balance of our personality is restored.

8 Dreams have access to 'complete memory'. Penfield's experiments definitely proved that no experience is lost from memory. Many dreams exhibit memories from earliest childhood – ones not known by the person, and only confirmed later. This includes memories dating from before birth.

9 Dreams 'incorporate ESP'. Whether we consider ESP to be the result of realisations arising from already held but unconscious material, or because some part of the mind transcends space and time, dreams certainly exhibit this function.

Without any exaggeration, if we can accept that the above are reasonable definitions of dream functions, and if coex gives access to the dream process while awake, then through it we have at our disposal a variety of tools, whether mental or physical, which we do not have otherwise. Linda and Su's examples show some of these possibilities in action. Through thinking in pictures we can often clarify a situation by bringing it down to its simplist factors that general thought left unclear. Cooperating with the self-regulating process enables us to more efficiently keep our health. Having the doorway to wider association of ideas enhances our creativity. Being able to bring to awareness parts of our memory usually lost in childhood, makes it possible to re-programme the gut level reactions which were imprinted on us in babyhood, which are frequently completely out of place in adult life. And the ESP faculty sometimes gives us the bonus of extending our awareness and gathering information helpful to work and life in general.

Because coex is based on two of the most universal and fundamental functions in humans – dreaming and the self-regulatory process – it has been available to human use throughout history. Although this has given rise to many different approaches there remain certain aspects which have to be similar. One of these is the need to have an open and allowing state of mind and body. Writing about this in relationship to problem solving in his commentary to the book *Secret of the Golden Flower*, Carl Jung says:-

> ...the essential urge to find a new way lay in the fact that the fundamental problem of the patient seemed insoluble to me unless violence was done to the one or the other side of his nature. I always worked with the temperamental conviction that in the last analysis there are no insoluble problems, and experience has so far justified me in that I have often seen individuals who simply outgrew a problem which had destroyed others. This 'outgrowing', as I called it previously, revealed itself on further experience to be the raising of the level of consciousness...
>
> Here and there it happened in my practice that a patient grew beyond the dark possibilities within himself, and the observation of the fact was an experience of the foremost importance to me. In the meantime I had learned to see that the greatest and most important problems of life are all fundamentally insoluble. They musy be so, because they express the necessary polarity inherant in every self-regulating system. They cannot be solved, but only outgrown. I therefore asked myself whether this possibility of outgrowing, or further psychic development, was not normal, while to remain caught in a conflict was something pathological. Everyone must posses that higher level [of possible growth], at least in embryonic form, and in favourable circumstances, must be able to develop the possibility. When I examined the way of development of those persons who, quietly, and as if unconsciously, grew beyond themselves, I saw that their fates had something in common. Whether arising from without or within, the new thing came to all those persons from a dark field of possibilities; they accepted it and developed further by means of it...
>
> What then did these people do in order to achieve the progress which freed them? As far as I could see they did nothing but let things happen...The art of letting things happen, action in non action, letting go of onself, as taught by Master Eckhart, became a key for me... The key is this: we must be able to let things happen in

the psyche. For us, this becomes a real art of which few people know anything. Consciousness is forever interfering, helping, correcting, and negating, and never leaving the simple growth of the psychic processes in peace. It would be a simple enough thing to do if only simplicity were not the most difficult of all things. It consists solely in watching objectively the development of any fragment of fantasy. Nothing could be simpler than this, and yet right here the difficulties begin. Apparently no fantasy fragment is at hand – yes there is one, but it is too stupid! Thousands of good excuses are brought against it: one cannot concentrate on it; it is too boring; what could come of it? It is 'nothing but', etc. The conscious raises prolific objections. In fact, it often seems bent on blotting out the spontaneous fantasy activity despite the intention, nay, the firm determination of the individual, to allow the psychic processes to go forward without intervention. In many cases there exists a veritable spasm of the conscious.

If one is successful in overcoming the initial difficulties, criticism is likely to start afterwards and attempt to interpret the fantasy, to classify, to aestheticize, or to depreciate it. The temptation to do this is almost irresistible. After a complete and faithful observation, free rein can be given to the impatience of the conscious; in fact it must be given, else obstructing resistances develop. But each time the fantasy material is to be produced, the activity of the conscious must be put aside.

In most cases the results of these efforts are not very encouraging at first. Moreover, the way of getting at the fantasies is individually different...oftentimes the hands alone can fantasise; they model or draw figures that are quite foreign to the conscious.

These exercises must be continued until the cramp in the conscious is released, or, in other words, until one can let things happen; which was the immediate goal of the exercise. In this way, a new attitude is created, an attitude which accepts the irrational and the unbelievable, simply because it is what is happening. The attitude would be poison for a person who has already been overwhelmed by things that just happen, but it is of the highest value for one who, with an exclusively conscious critique, chooses from the things that happen only those appropriate to his consciousness, and thus gets gradually drawn away from the stream of life into a stagnant backwater.

Very few people have written so powerfully, or with such insight as Jung has on the nature and practise of coex. That is why he has been quoted at such length. Also, some of the above statements are important to our understanding of what coex is and what it can do. It must be realised, however, that Reich and Jung were doctors, and so write on the subject from the viewpoint of dealing with illness or human problems. Coex is a great deal more than a doorway to the possibility of healing. As Jung himself mentions, it is also a way of growing beyond our present limitations, of finding 'more' in life. That more might be that we simply extend our awareness. A description given by David explains this.

I had learnt coex and, at first, used it to deal with personal problems. But as these became less pressing I discovered other possibilities in it. Tony had helped me to see that each of us pick up thousands of impressions from our environment without realising it. With that in mind, one day when I had a job to do two hundred miles away from home I used coex to check something out. I had agreed to mend someones flat roof. The job was not difficult, but needed a reasonably dry day. If I travelled two hundred miles and it rained, I would be well out of pocket. As the weather had been unsettled and with days of heavy rain, I asked my unconscious if it had any impressions on what the weather was likely to be in the area I needed to work. I allowed spontaneous images and feelings as I had learnt, and was amazed at the result. It was as if some part of my being was looking at the most immense forces. All the time they moved and shifted, with so much power I felt that if humans could harness one tiny part of them our energy needs would be solved. From the overall view my inner awareness then shifted and gave me the impression that there would be occasional light showers in the area I had asked about, nothing heavy enough to warrant not going. I was so impressed by the clarity and strength of the impressions, I drove to the job. While I worked there were a couple of showers as heavy clouds passed nearby, but nothing that delayed me or penetrated the uncovered roof.

I have myself frequently used coex to clarify or give more information on important situations. Part of the action of coex is to release to consciousness areas of our experience or impressions which may be relevant to our present needs, but which have remained unnoticed or forgotten. For instance, while working in Japan teaching coex, I was asked to show a young Japanese women how to use the technique. She was experiencing feelings of tension and discomfort in her chest, and could not understand their cause. Akiko was married to a Westerner and pregnant with their first child. As she allowed the spontaneous movements of coex she began coughing and choking. This continued for some time without change and I became puzzled as to what her body was expressing. When I asked her if she could feel what was behind her movements she shook her head. Wondering whether my unconscious had understood her body language I sought it's help. Straight-away a flow of impression and feelings arose which suggested that Akiko feared her husband would look for another woman after her child was born. I therefore suggested to her that the feeling in her chest was connected with her husband and the baby. She exploded into tears, as she had apparently been holding back that very fear for some time without expressing it.

In an attempt to understand where my unconscious had gathered this helpful piece of information I later explored the impressions. I saw that what had appeared to come almost magically to mind from nowhere was based on a forgotten sentence Akiko had spoken to me two days before about her coming baby. I had said that the baby would probably be quite a beautiful mixture of East and West. In a rather diffident voice she had said, "I hope so." At the time I had not attached any great importance to this mixture of words and feelings. Yet my unconscious had understood very well what she was saying.

As human beings we have a great many more possibilities in our lives than we presently use. Coex in action demonstrates that we have the ability to use faculties which often lie dormant. Whether the faculty is that of healing through a release of the self regulatory process; or whether it is that of bringing to consciousness information or realisations we had previously been unaware of, the act of allowing something to be experienced or known in body or mind, which was not evident there before, is fundamental. This bringing into operation what was previously only latent, is something we live with every moment of our lives. The everyday remembrance of how to walk and talk, of simple facts such as our telephone number, show how we constantly call into the arena of our awareness what is usually stored elsewhere. Words such as conscious and unconscious are sometimes made to appear very complex. When we connect them with memory though, it is obvious the experience we have gathered is never all at the one time in awareness. Only tiny parts of it are evident at any one moment. The rest is 'unconscious'. Also, between what we are aware of and what is unconscious there is a threshold. We can think of this as a screen of resistance which holds back the major part of what would otherwise flood into our awareness and cause massive confusion. To overcome this resistance a certain active force or procedure is necessary. Because this procedure is used so often we seldom notice what it is we do, but it is a little like a swinging door. When we hold a question in mind, or there is any call for information such as words to use in speech, we simply wait with a clear mind for the natural response we call memory to take place. In a similar way physical movements are a response to our motivation to walk or reach for something. So when we are actively thinking or willing something the 'door' swings from our consciousness to unconsciousness. What we thought or willed is then entered into our memory. If we then call upon our memory and wait with an open mind, the 'door' swings in the other direction to let the unconscious express its contents. It is upon this basic action of calling a response from our unconscious, that coex is founded.

It is quite easy to see that all of us have huge areas of our memory which we seldom or never use. But occasionally we may meet a school friend, or begin a conversation, which stimulates us to recall memories we thought long gone. Likewise there are areas of mind or body, the potential of which we hardly use. We need to remember also that because most of what emerges through the resistant screen of our 'threshold' is what we have sought or allowed, we may only build into our personality from within what appeals to us, what we like or agree with. This leads us to become one sided. In everyday terms it means that one person develops their intellect to the point where all of their views and decisions are dictated by it, while another person almost totally lives in their emotions or sexual drive. This may not be too important in terms of physical survival, but it can be extremely unhealthy in terms of our personality relating to the whole realm of biological, instinctual and life processes active with in us. In the quest for the things which they value as a personality, many people find themselves in direct conflict with what their body or the life in them wants. Having watched many people as they worked with coex, I have seen this battle between the life and the personality rage in a person's body, largely unconsciously. It has reminded me of national revolution, where a small elite – the intellectual government – rule the lives of millions of people who constitute the 'body' of a nation. If the government group have not listened to the needs of the body of their nation, then conflict arises. Worse still in personal terms, we miss awareness of much of our own potential and satisfaction. It matters not that we dub ourselves 'spiritual', 'conservationists' etc, if we have not taken the time to carefully allow our own being to speak to us, then we are one sided and out of touch.

These considerations made clear some of Jungs statements, and explain the rationale behind them. The 'dark possibilities within' are those aspects of ourself or our stored experiences which have not been allowed or encouraged to break through the threshold of resistance into conscious expression. They are dark because they are unconscious. 'Letting go of oneself' can also be seen as a rational necessity if we are to allow not only a balancing and healing of our personality, but also if we wish to contact the riches of what life in us knows. We have to 'let go' because otherwise the swinging door cannot open for the

25

unconscious to release its contents. The changed attitude of mind is as relevant as pushing in the clutch if we wish to change gear in a car. In other words, unless we understand the functions of our being, we cannot use it wisely or well. The open, non critical state of mind and body is the very first step in coex. The next step is to 'continue these exercises' of listening to the unconscious, 'until the cramp in the conscious is released'.

Although the simple use of the open-listening state of mind and body is sufficient for most people to establish communication with their inner resources, there are other factors which I have noticed are very important. These are to do with not only personal, but also cultural attitudes and concepts about the unconscious. Most people brought up in a western, Christian culture are deeply suspicious of the unconscious. We train ourselves and our children to remain in control of our feelings and drives to such a degree that to allow anything spontaneous is highly threatening. Many people I have worked with have said the same thing to me at the outset of learning coex. "But I don't know what is going to happen. How will I know if it is good or bad?"

This statement sums up the fears most people have about the unknown of their own nature. They want to know in advance what is going to emerge so that they can edit it, change it, or make it socially acceptable. I believe this shows a deep sense of not trusting ones own innate nature.

Something else many people say is, "But it might not make sense!" or "I don't know what to do." This suggests a sense of needing to have ready made ideas about what to do. During classes in which the people were asked to explore body movements, most people gave up after one minute or so. Some of these classes were ones in which the people had been exercising with 'given' movements weekly for many months. Yet after a class in which they were asked to discover their own spontaneous movements, several of the class dropped out and never returned. This I take to be an expression of an apprehension about anything new emerging into the persons life. Also, there is an element of these people not believing in their own power of discrimination to sort out what is useful for them. For myself, I have never found the unconscious to lie, but of course we can fool ourselves in projecting beliefs or hopes onto what it presents.

These anxieties, hopes, attitudes and expectations stand in the way of an easy and honest relationship with our inner process, just as they can stand in the way of an honest relationship between two people. In fact, the deepening of ones experience of coex is based upon the same factors as the deepening of a person to person relationship – trust, patience and an attempt to grow into further understanding and cooperation.

When I attempt to have an overall view of these different pieces of information pertaining to coex, then I see something which appears very important in human evolution. It seems quite clear that for millions of years the human animal lived without rational thought – which is a very recent thing – and they lived without what we call self awareness. Their actions did not arise out of thought as we know it, but out of a feeling response, a directive from the experience of their unconscious which had its own wisdom gathered from countless generations. This feeling or intuitive response was probably manifested in direct impulses to move, or in dream–like thought processes. The very tools of early writing were pictures, which probably indicates the mental life of those times. But as human beings developed a sense of personal identity, as they gave themselves personal and individual names, the ancient feeling sense, still obvious in such peoples as the Eskimos and Aborigines, was pushed out of use. When reasoning too became a common tool in human mental life, the seperation between the sense which had guided human life for millions of years, and the modern individual life was complete. Not only seperation but also division and even conflict. So we arrive at the dilemma of modern human beings who have a personality which is out of touch with major areas of its own being and unaware of its heritage of wisdom and problem solving faculties from the past. Therefore, I see the process of coex as a means of bringing about wholeness where there was division, integration in the place of the terrible weakness which selfconscious personality, being the veneer it is, has brought about.

CHAPTER 2

Honouring Yourself –
The Practice of Coex

When attempting to use coex we must remember that we are dealing with natural processes, and they have the possibility of entering into our conscious life when, and as they need. However, because of the way our personality relates to spontaneous drives, and perhaps also because of our social training as children, the self regulatory process of coex does not work spontaneously in most people. Nevertheless, the movements and techniques given in chapter three, and those about to be explained in this chapter, must be seen as exercises to re-establish our natural spontaneity. Therefore, when we use coex in a situation where we have chosen to apply it, to be clear, we need to recognise that we are choosing to allow it, or are 'practising' it rather than its emerging in its own way. Practising coex, or allowing it to emerge are both valid ways of experiencing it. The need to be clear about this point, however, arises from the fact that if we 'practise' coex, it will gradually begin to 'emerge' in ones life anyway, and that is natural and good.

Some examples will illustrate how this works in everyday life. But I want to set the scene a little to bring out certain aspects of what we will look at. So Peter and Adelaide, who we are going to consider, need to be seen as human animals. As physical animals they have certain very real needs such as a reasonable amount of food, air to breathe, and protection from the extremes of temperature. Physically they feel these needs and respond to their absence or their fulfillment. This response can be by feeling well and happy, or feeling ill and dying. But their organism as a whole responds in a whole range of ways to many more things than food, air and temperature. Having

conscious personalities which are named Peter and Adelaide extend this range of responses enormously, and also
make it more complex. For instance Peter's father may be
ill in hospital. At a physical level Peter's body was looked
after by his father while Peter was too young to fend for
himself. From purely basic animal kinship feelings Peter
has a drive to return that caring, but because of personality
clashes between the two males, Peter doesn't visit his
father while he is ill. He suppresses any feelings of wanting
to care with memories of past arguments.

In this situation Peter's psychological self-regulatory
process would attempt to find some sort of balance between the kinship drive and the hurt feelings in the personality. Biologically the kinship drive is more important
than a hurt pride, so the drive would attempt to be expressed into conscious life. If Peter had learnt to suppress
such feelings however, they would remain unconscious. If
Peter suppressed such attempts at self regulation over a
period of time, then a growing feeling of dis-ease would
occur, with Peter unaware of its cause.

That is purely a 'suppose' situation created to illustrate
how coex can be suppressed from spontaneous emergence.
But let us look at a real situation existing with Adelaide.
She is 42, a good looking woman with a strong drive
toward sex, (i.e. relating to a man, procreating, raising
children). Adelaide's mother recently died, and this
triggered an emotional breakdown, causing Adelaide to
withdraw from caring for her children, or caring for her
home or herself. Her husband left her during this period
and Adelaide found another man who lived with her.
Normal conversation was difficult with her because she
spoke on and on in a long blurt about sex, her children,
other people, her work. After a few months her new man
left her. Adelaide was hospitalised several times.

From the intensity and length Adelaide spoke about love
making, having a man, and suicide, her organism had very
powerful responses to these areas, yet her expression in
regard to them was not organismic. I mean that if an
organism, a cell, a creature, a human animal, is hurt or
pleasured, it responds in a physical way and with obvious
feelings. The reaction might be sexual erection, deep
sobbing or any other straight response. But Adelaide's was

almost wholly verbal. This suggests that Adelaide had a powerful suppression on her self regulatory process, preventing the experience of emotions flowing from her real inner fears and pains. Yet why would a person suppress the very things which would balance their being and bring about greater ease?

The answer could be linked with how Adelaide is structured as a personality, and how her personality relates to the processes of her body. Clues to this lie in her age, that her breakdown occurred after her mothers death, and her preoccupation with procreation. One of her statements was that the man she lived with couldn't give her a baby, and this was the only real form of love. So we can see that the structure of her personality is deeply bound up with being capable of childbirth. That she is 42, faced with losing her procreative ability, confronted by death and the loss of two men, must not only threaten to destroy her personality as it is, but cause many inner responses to occur which she is not allowing to be expressed. If she allowed the responses to emerge into consciousness, she, Adelaide, would have to meet and integrate the very facts of life she most rejects – meet them WITHIN HERSELF!!!

Peter is in his late forties in his second marriage, and has attempted to honour coex in his life for some years. What follows is his description of how coex emerges into his life spontaneously now. "After some years of gradually learning to let myself meet the sort of feelings I used to hold inside, I now meet coex in quite gentle yet effective ways. For instance this morning I woke feeling good, but knowing that I needed sexual meeting with my wife Eileen. When I got close to her though I could feel her withdrawal and lack of physical excitement, so I didn't push my need. As I was dressing the conversation revolved around how Eileen related to her first husband, – a topic she initiated – and how we were relating – initiated by myself. We had not reached any satisfactory conclusion by the time I was ready to start the day by visiting the post office, and I left feeling I wasn't going to be pulled down by her mood, and determined to be independent. As I left I had an uneasy feeling inside. I started to push it down but realised that my attitude to Eileen only satisfied my independent self, and there was another part of me which was upset by what had happened. By the time I was walking back from the post office the feeling was clear enough for me to see that although it was fine to be independent, I was attempting to acheive it at the expense of my feelings of care and connection I had built with Eileen over the years. When I arrived back Eileen was sitting playing with her granddaughter. She looked okay but I went to her, hugged her and said, 'It's a big world out there, and I don't want to go it alone.' Tears sprang to her eyes, so I saw she had been trying to play silly buggers just as I had. Then the tension which had existed between us vanished.

Maybe that sounds like a very small incident, but I know that in the past I let those small things mount up until they were huge grudges inside. Now I can allow the feelings which arise, and so I let my whole self have a say in how I live, instead of being the sort of dictator I used to be.

The simplest way of allowing coex to enter our life is to honour what we feel. While working therapeutically with a man – Andy – recently, one of the common errors connected with this was demonstrated to me again. Andy had allowed spontaneous movements and feeling while working alone, and had arrived at a sense of confusion and failure. In his words, "I feel blitzed". When I asked him to explain what he meant he said that he just couldn't do whatever was necessary to succeed with coex, and felt devastated. In other words, Andy was looking for a feeling of success and confidence as the thing he should have found. When I suggested he allow himself to experience the 'blitzed' feeling instead of searching elsewhere, he cried with real emotion, and could directly see how the feelings were related to his childhood when he was put in an orphanage. In his very search he had been avoiding the things most meaningful by only wanting to see the positive side of himself. Allowing the tears enabled him to acknowledge how important his 'orphanage' feelings were influencing his life. Letting them be felt was the beginning of their integration into his conscious life. This integration would let them grow and change instead of being locked unconsciously into him in the same form they were in his childhood.

Honouring Our Feeling Sense

Apart from our well-known five senses such as seeing and hearing, we have other senses, equally as well-known to us through experience, but seldom mentioned or defined. We have a sense of balance, a moral sense, a musical sense and a feeling sense. When using coex the feeling sense is particularly important, and the experiences of Peter and Andy show how this sense worked for them. Long before the development of language in the human race, or in our childhood, the feeling sense was the urge or means by which the complexities of life were dealt with. When we watch animals in the wild deal with difficult situations and survive without being able to think as we do, it is obvious how practical the feeling sense is. It becomes understandable when we remember that most of our memories and experience are unconscious. Also, many impressions we gather, and many of our mental functions such as cross referencing information, take place outside our waking awareness. Information arising from these sources and expressing itself through the feeling sense has been given a variety of names such as hunches, intuition, presentiment, and so forth. Obviously, what some people call premonition or a hunch is simply their own anxieties or prejudices. My mother-in-law, before I married my second wife, told us she had experienced an intuitive insight that our marriage would only last eighteen months before it failed. Our marriage is now in its seventh year.

Most of us though have correct hunches arising from our feeling sense. Such hunches or insights can be about our own internal psychology, such as Peter and Andy experienced, or about any aspect of our life. Years ago, while I was running a book business and was only beginning to learn how to use my feeling sense, I read a book about Edgar Cayce. For two days I had a powerful urge to write to people who were continuing his work in America, and make contact with them. I did this but still the feeling persisted. It subsided only when I wrote again and offered the services of my book business if they needed it. A week later two letters arrived from Virginia Beach. The one with the earliest postmark explained the work of the organisation – A.R.E. – and then asked if I knew of someone who would stock their books, as they had a lecture tour planned, and needed someone to act as agent for them. The second letter simply said, "We must be working a fine case of telepathy here. Thanks. The books are on their way, and our lecturer, Col. Adams, will arrive soon." The results are seldom that dramatic, but are nevertheless generally helpful.

Memories and processes occuring outside verbalisation and conscious thinking, have often never been shaped into words or clear concepts. Therefore, they cannot be conceptualised – but they can be FELT! Our subtle feelings and senses enable the unconceptualised material to be presented to our conscious mind. Feelings form a link between our thinking, verbal self, and the deep unconscious self. If, like my mother-in-law in her response to my marrying her daughter, one is the victim of ones feelings and anxieties rather than the observer of them, hunches are confusing rather than helpful. But there are very clear techniques which enable us to meet our feeling sense in a constructive way. These techniques form an excellent introduction to the 'practice' of coex.

NONE OF THE FOLLOWING METHODS ARE 'BETTER' OR 'WORSE' THAN ANY OF THE OTHERS. I THEREFORE SUGGEST YOU TRY THEM IN THE ORDER EXPLAINED, AND FIND WHICH MOST SUIT YOUR NEEDS AND ENVIRONMENT.

Discovering the Seed of Growth

There are exercises of mind and body one needs to practise to develop acquaintance with the feeling sense. Each of us has a feeling sense, but often we have not developed it or learnt to use it consciously. So these exercises are rather like an artist learning to use their sight for their art. Eugene Gendlin, in his excellent book FOCUSING, (Bantam Books) calls it the 'felt sense', and says that it is what we experience before we speak. We seldom know beforehand the words we are going to use, except in a formal situation, but we do have a 'felt sense' of what we are going to say. This then becomes verbalised when we say it. Also, if we think of two friends, and move from one to the other in our mind, we have a feeling sense of how different each one is. We have these feeling responses about everybody we meet, everything we think, and everything we do. They underly our whole life, but very often we fail to notice them. In the following exercises we are going to spend time considering, exploring and learning to work with them.

To begin this first practice you need to create the right setting and situation. You need to wear comfortable clothes which you can easily move and relax in. Take your shoes off, put a blanket on the floor area you choose to practice on, and clear a space big enough for you to stretch out in and spread arms and legs. Create a space in time also. It is important to give yourself about half an hour without other pressing issues to properly meet your inner feelings. Drop self criticism and give yourself permission to express sounds and movement freely.

When you are ready to begin, stand or lie in the centre or your space and raise you arms above your head. Hold them so they are quite extended. Then bring to mind the idea or image of an unplanted seed. It can be any sort of seed. Now notice whether your body in its present posture feels as if it is expressing the form and condition of the seed. The aim is to consider how you and your body feel in relationship to the idea and sense you have of the seed. Many people find, for instance, that having the arms extended does not 'feel' like an unplanted seed. Do not struggle with this. It is just an experiment, play with it, have fun. So if you do not feel your being is expressive of the seed, move about, explore different postures until you begin to feel more satisfied. Explore in this way until you feel you have found a position which is right. Take your time. Notice whether the arms and head are right. Would a seed which is not growing feel alert, sleeping, waiting? See if you can find an inner feeling which for you feels like a seed. Do not attempt to think the whole thing out or consider it scientifically. Let whatever feeling sense you have guide you. If you get lost, come back to arms and legs extended and spread and again consider whether that FEELS like a dry unplanted seed. If not, work with that feeling of 'not right' until it gets to be 'right'.

When you find a position and inner feeling which suits you, take the next step by letting yourself explore, in just the same way, what happens when the seed is planted in warm moist soil and begins to grow. Continue your feeling exploration to find out what will occur when the seed grows, puts out leaves, blossoms and fulfills its cycle. Explore the whole cycle of the seed's expression. Don't hold a rigid idea of what the growth of the seed means. What we are looking for is that you explore your own feeling sense in regard to the thought of the seed's growth. It might be that as the seed you feel very strongly you do not want to grow. In which case simply remain in the form of the seed until you feel a change and an urge to grow, or until your session time is up.

Not only is this an exercise for our feeling sense, but it is also a way the process of coex can be expressed. The concept of the seed structures what happens, but it is still a channel in which self regulation can occur. You can consider it a successful coex experience if some aspect of what arises is spontaneous or unexpected. Even if the unexpected does not emerge in the first session, it will do so as you learn to let go of thinking and critical appraisal of what is happening, and leave the body open to free expression. So at first it doesn't matter if the session feels mechanical and contrived. Having those feelings means you are sensing what is happening, and you can thereby refine your technique with their help. By letting go of the controlling urge, you can let the spontaneous and creative part of you express itself.

It is helpful to use this form of coex once or twice a week for a full half hour or longer each time. What happens may differ each time, for the unconscious is very creative. In symbols, or in direct experience, something of your own nature will be expressed in the drama of growing. As you practice, any stiffness of feelings or hesitancy will lessen. The theme of what emerges will become clearer and more fully felt. As this happens you can use different starting points. Instead of the seed, use the image of WATER, of AIR, of EARTH, or the SUN. Just thinking about them they may seem very abstract, but my experience is that very few people are unable to enter into them quite deeply through their feeling sense and coex.

Judith, who teaches a yoga class, describes her use of this approach to coex as follows:

> . . .I felt as if I were the bud of a crocus. I seemed to be slowly unfolding with difficulty. Not until I fully opened did I feel a great relief. The results of this have made me feel very positive in my outlook, and far happier. . .I am a trainee yoga teacher and have been teaching for three years. I have a small class of fourteen students who are keen and attend regularly. I decided to have my students try coex to see how they would react. I explained it as well as I could, and the feedback I got was:– A man in his thirties said, 'I felt I was in a womb. It was very comfortable, cosy and dark. I wanted to stay there. I didn't want to come away – it was so peaceful. I have never experienced anything like it before.' He was very impressed. A woman in her thirties felt like throwing her arms around and kicking her legs. 'I felt I wanted to give birth and was about to deliver.' She didn't fling herself about, but held back. I think it was a pity she didn't let go. Perhaps I didn't explain the whole procedure clearly enough for them to understand that it was entirely free movements. The majority acted out being flowers. Only one in the class thought it was a lot of 'bloody rubbish', her words. She didn't even try. She thought she would feel stupid acting out a seed. I personally was surprised at the outcome; that so much should happen first time.

When using the starting point of the seed, or water, etc, we are giving the unconscious a ready made structure to work with. Because we may be unfamiliar with a completely unstructured approach to our inner processes, such a structure gives at least some sense of familiarity and confidence. Even so, some people find they want everything fully described, scripted or choreographed. The very point of coex, however, is to begin moving beyond the known in ourselves, towards creative newness and the unexpected. So even if some anxiety is felt, as with the woman Judith describes who defends her anxiety of the unknown by calling the exercise 'bloody rubbish', one needs to gradually move beyond such resistant feelings.

With the structured approach one also needs to leave the

result open ended. With the man described in Judith's group, for instance, although he started with the structure of the seed, his experience was one of being in a womb, in a peaceful feeling state, and the woman felt as if she was about to give birth. With a large enough sample, the results would be enormously varied. Many people would go through the whole cycle of the plant's life; some would find they grew to a certain place and stopped; some would have no impulse to grow at all; some would move quickly from the seed structure to personal feelings. So in your own practice leave yourself open to what emerges. If you stay with the seed and its growth that's fine, but if you find your inner process diverging, let it express what it wants to.

If Feelings are a New World

Eugene Gendlin suggests exercises which are less active physically than the seed structure, and are helpful if you are uncertain whether you have feelings or not. People often tell me that they are not sure if what they are observing in themselves is a feeling or a thought, and Gendlin's approach is helpful. He suggests:–

1 When in a time of quiet, think of something or someone you love or think is beautiful. It can be a pet, an object, a person, anything. Consider why you love what you have chosen, or why it is beautiful.

2 Notice what different feelings arise in you, how your body feels, when you consider what you have chosen, than when you think of something else.

    I find it helpful to think of the body as a T.V. screen you are watching. Before you think about your beautiful thing, notice what tensions or peace are on the screen. Take note of any aches and pains, any sense of tiredness or energy, and any attitudes such as boredom, or being pleased, which are there. Don't try to banish these, just note them. Then bring to mind your chosen object and note what changes take place on the screen of your being.

3 See if you can find any words which fit what you can observe or feel. Let yourself feel what the words are about,

and note whether what is on your screen changes, and what it is expressing.

A series of exercises I devised which help to define this important feeling sense, is an extension of considering oneself as a screen. With a similar sort of setting as used for the seed exercise, stand and relax unnecessary tension. Take note of what is then happening on ones 'screen'. Simply note, do not alter. Then think of a word such as ashamed. Hold the word in your mind and note what changes occur on the 'screen', and what changes there are in body posture. Give this some minutes, then change the word to unashamed and note the difference. Try this with different words such as depressed/happy, failure/success, etc.

Most people, but not everyone, can find an easily noticeable change with the different words. Even the body posture alters. And the exercise not only helps us to note the different feeling qualities we have with each word, but also demonstrates how just holding a thought can alter our whole body and feeling situation.

Because the ability to consciously verbalise or be able to clearly think about what one is considering, is the last and integrating stage in levels of awareness, it is important to express what one experiences in these experiments. I believe a good test of integration is when what one describes is understandable not only to oneself, but also to any casual listener. For some people the word and the feeling are very much connected. Something which is very important is that when we look at the 'screen' and note what is happening, some parts of what are being experienced will be clear and easily put into words. But there will also be an area which is not yet clear, not yet capable of being expressed. You are looking into a place in yourself which is beyond words. If you continue to observe it, however, it begins to open up, to grow, as it were, and gradually becomes clear enough to join with words. That is the most important area. In watching it we are looking into the unconscious. When it 'opens' the unconscious emerges into consciousness where it can be verbalised. WHEN YOU ALLOW THE FREE EXPRESSION OF COEX

TO UNITE WITH THE OBSERVATION OF THE WORDLESS PLACE IN
YOURSELF, A NEW AND WONDERFUL LIFE SKILL HAS BEGUN.
The process of coex can begin to release into consciousness
important experiences which were previously unavailable.
Our observation of the place beyond words allows a
communication between our deep unconscious and our
conscious sense of self. If these exercises in contacting the
feeling sense are used, and the greater facility in this area is
brought into the seed approach to coex, a much fuller
experience will result.

The Unstructured Approach

Because there are so many facets to human nature, ranging
from nameless anxieties to insights into the nature of life,
any structure we place on coex may limit it. I have noticed
with groups which approach coex from a particular standpoint, such as psychotherapy or religion, that although the
basic functioning is the same, the experience in the group
is largely within that heading. In Primal Therapy for
instance, even when the feelings arising are spontaneous
and unexpected, they are nearly always about childhood
pain. In Subud groups however, which are part of a spiritual brotherhood, although the activity is obviously self
regulatory, what arises is mostly idealistic and to do with
moral development. Barter for example, describing his
early experiences in Subud, says it was like being baptised
in a flow of water. Participants in Primal Therapy describe
their experiences as reliving the pain of being born, etc.

W.V. Caldwell, writing about the findings arising from
LSD psychotherapy says:

> The kaleidoscopic patterns and heightened sensory per-
> ceptions; the sumptuous and exotic fantasies that seem
> to bear no personal application, the symbolic myths and
> rituals that do; the experiences of fusion, Samadhi, and
> psychosis; the physiological urges to squeeze, or bite, or
> throw; the passage of protoplasmic disorganization; the
> historical recalls of childhood; the splendid religious and
> philosophical revelations – how can one make sense of
> them all? If the psychedelic experience had confirmed

the theories of Freud, or Jung, or anybody else we might have been relieved. Instead it has confirmed them all and added a few more besides.

We must beware of putting any rigid conceptual framework onto what it is to be a human being, especially in regard to our unconscious life. If we feel naked and anxious without such firm theories, then by all means use what is necessary. But recognise at least that your approach will limit what you allow yourself to find. It is easy to see that our being spans the distance between solid physical substances, such as our bones, to the most extraordinary subtleties of mind. All of these are ourself. Opening to only a part of what we are is to miss a great deal of the wonder.

The approach to coex in this unstructured form needs the same sort of approach we used in the structure of the seed – i.e. sufficient floorspace, etc. You start by standing in the middle of your floorspace, giving yourself the same sort of time and attitude as before. This time, instead of holding your arms above your head as with starting the seed, start by circling the arms. Take the arms above the head, down the opposite sides of the body with the arms fully extended, then upward crossing the front of the trunk. In the full movement the hands are then forming wide circles which cross the front of body. This arm circling, just like the arms stretched above the head in the structured approach, is simply to help you begin coex. Dispense with it as soon as you can allow coex without it.

Meanwhile, circle the arms with the eyes closed and bring your awareness to the shape your hands are making in space. As you become aware of the shapes the hands are carving, watch what feelings you have as to how you would like to move. Give yourself permission to 'doodle', to make any sort of shapes your feelings or body incline you to. Allow any sort of posture or movement, as active or quiet as you like. Allow sounds to accompany the movements if there is an urge to make them, and allow whatever feelings accompany them. Hold the attitude that what you are doing doesn't have to make sense. Nor does it have to comply with what other people might expect of you. Realise that you are allowing another part of yourself, perhaps a non-verbal part, or a facet unknown to the rational mind, to express. With a non-critical watching attitude, relax and let your body and feeling sense direct what happens. There is no need to fiercely concentrate in order to wipe the mind clear of other influences. But you may need to relax the part of the mind which always needs to know beforehand what you are going to do. This is not like creative dance, in which there may exist a need to produce something pleasing for others to watch. With coex you need an open area in which your being can make its own adjustments, and movement and feeling has a chance to express itself outside rational criticism and demands of everyday life.

Give yourself at least half on hour in which to explore what spontaneous movements and feelings emerge. Below is a summary of what may happen in this practice.

1 Although the movements may at first appear haphazard and irrational, if you allow them to continue without criticism, they usually express – perhaps only over a period of several sessions – a particular theme or point.

2 Like a dream, the theme or drama often symbolises ones life situation, or something within oneself, such as the remaining emotions or attitudes from past experience, or a creative realisation. Or the movements may be expressive of the body's own need to release energy or mobilise itself and its urges.

3 There are obvious stages or depths to the experience. Movement is often the first. Feelings and fantasy can then combine with the movement. Only with a few people do they occur without each other. If met in the right way these can lead to insight into what is being expressed. In other words the symbolic movements, if that is what they are, can give way to rational understanding. This is not because one has thought out a plausible explanation for what happens. An example given by Barbara will make this plain.

For several sessions in the group I was practising with, my hands had made complicated movements as if I were making something. I realised as I observed that my hands were working at something, operating on someone in a healing way. As this happened I had strong sensations of energy and feelings streaming along my arms into my hands. There was a woman in our group who had cataracts of the eyes, and what my hands were doing was a psychic or spiritual healing on her eyes. The physical sensations and feelings were strong enough to make me wonder what would happen. I didn't tell the woman, but watched to see if her eyes improved. Each week the same thing occurred, but the woman's eyes did not improve. This left me with the question, 'What on earth am I doing?' Leaving this question in mind I allowed the thing to continue. As I was watching it during the session straight after I had considered the question I suddenly had a memory of my teenage years, when I read a lot of books about spiritual healing. I felt again something of the intensity of desire which I had felt in wanting to be a healer myself. Suddenly the answer popped into my head. My urge to heal had set up a message in my unconscious to satisfy my ideals. There was something like a 'programme' in me which diverted some of my energies toward healing, or at least, acting it out. As soon as I realised what was happening my hands stopped their movements and they never occurred again. Up until that point I had thought my inner self was lying to me. It was saying I could heal when I couldn't. But with the new understanding I realised it wasn't lying at all. It was simply expressing energy in ways I had set up in the past. That such expression was non-realistic had now become evident, and so I could let go of that old pattern.

Barbara's description shows that her understanding came out of observation, a 'floating' – not a forcefully searched – question, and by allowing the continuing process to respond to her question. Also, what she says illustrates another point about coex. Namely that some themes in coex express habitual patterns of energy use or attitudes. For instance if we have a habitual pattern of turning our anger inwards, our coex movements or theme might express as banging our own chest aggressively. Our awareness of such habits enables us to begin changing them.

4 The basic action in our sessions is self regulatory. In these movements, themes and fantasies, our organism attempts its own healing and balancing. But a part of self regulation is the process of physical and/or psychological growth. So some parts of what emerge are to do with adding to our psychic experience and stature.

5 The process is amenable to direction. It is a learnt skill, allowing the unconscious to express in a way that is meaningful and integrative with consciousness. Some of the possibilities of this direction will be explained in other chapters.

6 What arises, if we are open, comes from many facets of ourselves. Overall there is a uniting of the light and dark sides of ourselves. Caldwell describes this as follows:

> [One person,] looking for herself, came upon a tightly closed box. Tearing it open – in her fantasy – she found inside a lovely rose, and realised that she had been enclosed in a box of puritanism, of self denial and physical shame. The outer petals of the rose, pink and mauve, seemed to whirl and dance; they sent her fancy spinning off like a ballerina into flowered landscapes of delicious femininity. The inner petals were shaded from the light, obscure and mysterious. Here the colours darkened to deep crimson and velvet purple. They reflected her deep animality. These she avoided, until she realised that it took both the light and the dark to make a lovely rose. She could not have one without the other. Gradually the rose became a nourishing symbol in her life and growth.

Two's a Power Greater Than One

Anyone who has practised coex alone and then has the chance to experience it with another person, or other people with whom they feel safe, knows what tremendous amplification or added power is brought to it. Such a person or group need to have the same absence of destructive criticism and judgement, the same open curiosity that one brings to oneself in the practice. When this happens you may be able to enter areas of experience previously closed.

Even though I have been using coex for many years, having a good partner or group who will witness my work is still an enormous stimulus.

A simple way to work in a group of two or more is to find a room or space that is suitable and start off just as one would if practising alone. Use the arm circling if you have never practised coex before – or if you can allow coex easily, start by standing together for a few moments to drop what has been happening in everyday life. Get into the feeling of an open body and non-judgement. Then stand apart and allow coex for the time alloted. This format can handle a group of two or a hundred. Size doesn't matter. But by having other people with you, a good environment in which the action of coex can express itself is formed through mutual support. In such a setting it does not matter if very little or a great deal happens. Being in close proximity to other people allowing coex is helpful even if little outwardly occurs. It establishes in one the realisation that people can allow the irrational and be none the worse afterwards. So a sense of trust in ones own unconscious builds. For some people coex will not occur until this trust is established, so they may need an ongoing group which will allow them to witness coex in action.

Ursula began reasonably quickly, practising with Krysia who had learnt coex in a group with myself. She here describes her first three sessions:

The first time we met I was active in a pleasant mild way with the odd disturbance thrown in.

The second time was also quite contained and at the end I sat as in a meditation but aware of what was going on around me. Then Krysia came to me to let me know time was up. She knelt before me. I did not move. She touched me and it was like a dam breaking and release happened. I cried a strange cry. As I cried I was happy to the same measure as I was sad I had well-being in me to the same degree I was involved in it.

The coex after that started with yawning which could not be satisfied no matter how much the body helped the momentum of the yawn, or how loud the sighs were. Then the yawns became shouts and screams. I wanted to give the final yawn as I did not see much sense in spending an hour yawning. But then came a final piercing scream which only vaguely seemed to come from me; as I heard it more than did it. As it happened I was no longer looking out of the window of that room, but saw my mother's portrait etched against the window, as I saw her once when I was a child. She was fighting an angina attack and screaming with pain, losing control of her body functions and senses almost. Then I broke into sobs and tears. Strange sobs to me, as I felt all the panic, yet all compassion, all the lies with which she held me, the negative lies, and I felt love for her too. Yet I was also watching myself sobbing; 'Oh mum. Oh mum.' And 'Let go. Let Go.' And later I felt freed and quiet after the storm. As my hands smoothed over my body it felt so good. As the sound 'U' came out on breathing deeply it made a warm vibation in the small of my back which radiated up to the ribs and down to the tailbone. During the period of quiet which followed I saw that place in me filled with light. I was coated in the light, and a counterpart of me, made of light, penetrated me and extended beyond me. I also felt my posture in that area had changed and I had no more difficulty with being comfortable in certain sitting positions.

Ursula managed to allow herself greater freedom of expression in just three sessions. Although she was applying judgement to her yawns, she nevertheless allowed them until they became sounds which incorporated feelings. Her flowing enegy could then clear a source of stress which had remained in her for years. When that cleared Ursula was able to allow feelings of pleasure which incorporated a sense of light. The result of this was an immediate change in her posture.

Another way of working is with just one partner, where one allows coex and the other withnesses. Although this may sound little different to the way Ursula was practising, where both people allow coex, in use there is a great difference. The witness acts as an unspoken question which stimulates our process to respond more fully. It is the format most often used in therapeutic situations, and in groups such as Co-Counselling. Its advantages are that the witness can give feedback to the worker, and with experience, can point out what the worker may have missed. But perhaps the fundamental strength is that when we have someone elses attention our being is much more expressive. After all, it is the basic form in which communication takes place. Even if one regularly works with a therapist using Gestalt or Co-Counselling approach, I find it an advantage to bring to them the freedom of movement and expression coex allows.

During a recent course I taught, I took advantage of being able to work with a partner and had a very helpful session with Barry, one of the students. Afterwards he said he had felt helpless at times because he didn't know what to do or what to say. From my point of view that wasn't true at all. Just by being there Barry had been a great help. Also, at no point did he judge what I was doing as good or bad. I felt an active sympathy and involvement from him, and that was enough. However, learning creative listening can aid the process still further. So below some useful points are listed.

A There is no need to respond to what the worker says or does. It is their work session. They are working on themselves. Your main function is to witness, so do not be tempted to begin a conversation. In one class in which I was teaching creative listening, Di, a rather motherly woman, could not stop herself responding every time her partner spoke. Di had years of caring motherhood behind her, and she couldn't get out of the role. So when her partner said something like, "Last week I had a real bust up with my wife", Di would respond with something like, "What a pity. You shouldn't row with your wife like that. It doesn't do any good".

Such responses are highly judgemental and are value judgements at that. If you are on the receiving end of such comments, they either irritate or lead you to feel you do not wish to expose your inner life to such a person.

B Some of the most helpful responses are: 1. A summary of what the worker did physically given at opportune times. Thus you might say, 'At first you were quite still, then you crumpled to the ground.' If you can gain an impression of what such movements describe in a dramatic sense that is helpful too. So in the already stated movements we might add, 'When you crumpled I felt you were expressing despair. You remained quiet for a while then got up with what seemed like a new strength.' If such information is given as an opinion rather than a fact, it allows the worker to find their own response, and to see whether it fits their experience. 2. A statement of any overall theme you notice. So you might say, 'Many of the movements you made were backwards as if retreating.' Or, 'Almost all you said seemed to have a note of complaint, as if you felt a victim.' While using coex there is no need for the worker to respond to these comments as in a conversation. It is enough to hear them and let their inner process respond.

C Questions are a very powerful tool in such a relationship and should be used with great care. If a worker is in the middle of a session in which subtle feelings are emerging, and you suddenly ask, 'Has this got something to do with your mother? this could draw them straight into an intellectual consideration of the question, inviting them to respond verbally. It would be much better to put the information as a suggesion, such as, 'My feeling is that this has something to do with your mother.' This does not call for an immediate response and so allows the worker to carry on with their experience.

D Beware of preconceived opinions about what the worker is dealing with. I remember in one of my early experiences as a witness the worker, a woman, kept rubbing her vagina. I felt sure it must have something to do with a repressed urge to masturbate. Fortunately I kept my opinion to myself, and it turned out to be childbirth. If we do get stuck in an opinion, and pin it on the worker, it can cause a powerful conflict between what is arising within them, and what we are pushing on them from outside. It helps to remember that our opinions on what someone else is experiencing are just that, OPINIONS. With experience our statements can be enormously helpful, but not until we have learnt some humility and discipline.

E There are important questions, however, and these should be used at the end of a session. For instance, if the

47

session is symbolic in some way, it is helpful to ask what the worker feels it expresses. For instance they may act out being locked up in a small space, and when asked for opinions of what it expresses, say it feels just like their work situation, where they feel stifled and cramped. Having moved from a symbol to a life situation the next step is to ask the worker to explore via coex how they might satisfyingly get out of the trap. At first this might once more be in symbols, but can be brought into every-day terms by discussion.

If the worker uncovers an area of childhood experience that was painful, or any other important event, it is bound to have left certain habit patterns in them. Even when the stress of the event has been released, the habits will remain unless made conscious. Eddie had released the shock of being put in a hospital and separated from his mother at three. He went on to re-enact the scene where his mother used the threat of putting him in a 'home' in order to make him obedient. The tensions had been released, but when Eddie was asked what the experience left him with, how it influenced his life 'now', he discovered previously un-conscious habits. Namely, he had made an unconscious decision as a child never to trust a woman with his love again. This meant that in his marriage Eddie always kept a lot of his feeling cut off from his wife to avoid the possibility of getting hurt again, as he was in childhood. Being aware of this pattern enabled Eddie to gradually take the risk of sharing more of himself with his wife.

Therefore the questions need to lead **1.** from symbols to insight. **2.** From past experience to what habits the experience left. **3.** From the awareness of the habit(s) to a re-assesment of what the person wants to do with that part of themselves now.

F If the worker contacts feelings which are not clear, they need to look at what they are experiencing to see if they can recognise having felt it at any time in their life. Andy, mentioned at the beginning of this chapter his unclear 'blitzed' feelings became clear when he saw them as results of being in an orphanage. One cannot always make this sort of connection with feelings, but if you can it integrates them much faster.

G Discussion of the session is useful in nearly every case, whether as witness and worker, or as a co-practising group. It helps to clarify and define what occurred. It also means the person exposes to other people what may have been hidden even from themselves, which in a sympathetic setting can be healing.

The Seed Group

The structured seed approach can be used in a group form as well as alone. In group form it has a slightly different framework and a lot more possibilities than when practised alone. It needs three or four people, with or without experience of coex. It is best if at least one person has used coex though, and probably best if each person has used the 'alone seed' at least once.

To start the group, one of the members chooses to be the Seed. This person is the worker. The other members take on the roles of earth and water. But these latter roles are only loose guides, and I am not suggesting any attempt to act them out rigidly should be made. Basically they are witnesses, but in a slightly different form to the one-to-one work. Whoever is the Seed starts by standing in the middle of the others, who take time to make contact with her/him. They allow time to find an attitude which enables them to get closer physically and emotionally than in usual social roles. So without forcing or acting mechanically, the members touch and draw near to the Seed. When this is established the Seed curls up on a prepared space – with blanket or cushions – on the floor. The members draw near and make contact again. Get close, cover the Seed's body with theirs, penetrate with their touch, as does earth and water.

As a guide to this, it is helpful to consider in human terms, if you are in the water role, how you would penetrate the seed to stimulate its growth process? If you are in the earth role, again in human terms, how would you relate to the seed to give it a medium in which or from which to grow? If you are in the seed role, then you allow your spontaneous reaction to this. Allow the process of coex to move you without considering what you should do. Trust your inner process. The group is an intimate one. It has many dimensions of experience possible. Not only is it a meeting of people in a way not usually possible socially, but it is also a place to learn human contact, how to give caring and support to another human being, and how to communicate with others non-verbally.

Because there are so many different ways people experience the seed group, I will quote a few responses:

I've never been with people in that way before. I think it was the first time I really relaxed with a group. — When I was the seed I didn't have any urge to move or grow at all. At first this worried me. I kept wondering if the others would be bored or disappointed. When I told them, the worry disappeared; they were all just enjoying being close. — Being the helper was great. I got so much pleasure from supporting and being near the Seed and the others in the group. But when it was my turn to be the Seed I didn't enjoy that at all. I felt restless and claustrophobic and quickly pulled out. It has made me realise for the first time in my life that I find it difficult to receive that sort of closeness from others. I have to be the giver. — Until I became the seed I had never realised how hungry I was to have other people near me. I wanted to hold and touch in a way I had never allowed myself before. Since then it has been easy for me to hold people, babies, my wife, with more giving than I could in the past. — First I was just curled up. I felt comfortable, and relaxed into coex while the others completely covered my body with theirs. It really was like being planted. After a while a flicker of movement arose pushing my head out. This came in waves, increasing in strength, until my head was pushing out and up like a plant growing. I didn't try to think what I ought to do, just went with the pleasure of it. In the early stages this didn't seem to involve the others, although I could feel them close. But by the time I was up on my knees there was such pleasure flowing through me, such joy at being close, being able to feel the soft skin of a face against mine, that my pleasure involved the others. It is the nearest thing to making love without sex I have ever come across. I felt all the flow, the contact, without in any way going into areas that are unacceptable. When I was standing, growing from the sheer energy of movement welling up from within, we all seemed to be one moving, living process. I felt I had given something of myself to the others without saying one word. And I also experienced them as distinct qualities around me. At the end I could sit with them for a long time, holding hands, head on them, without the need to speak.

Although we start with the structure of the seed and its growth, you do not need to stay within that structure if your own experience takes you out of it. Some people feel they are a baby being born. Others have a direct here and now relationship with the group which needs to be explored. But basically one is setting up the group as an environment in which to allow coex to occur. The coex action might take up the seed image and use it, or express it in another way. Because other people are so near, what emerges may be quite different to what arises alone. Like the person who found it difficult to receive, ones theme might be about the difficulty or pleasure in relating to others.

The notes given about the creative listening or witnessing also apply with the seed group. As a helper we are supporting the Seed in their work. The Seed is the one to say when they are ready to finish the session, but as a witness you may be able to give them an assisted passage by careful feedback. Also, discussion and feedback are important at the end of each session. There is a great deal to learn about ourself, the way we relate, and what emerged in the seed group. It is an unusual social setting and we may have reached beyond boundaries we usually erect. To know how others felt about you laughing, touching, not moving, expressing deep feelings, etc, is vital to your realistic appraisal of future relationships. Again, this is something which although important, we do not experience often enough. The experience of Jane quoted below shows another side of the need to complete, through discussion and careful witnessing, what began in a non-verbal way.

When I got back – from the seed group – I felt quite ill, and dragged around for a few weeks feeling like death. I even went to the doctor, but all he could find was mild anaemia. This feeling developed into a period of absolutely compulsive eating, with an awful feeling of never feeling satisfied by what I ate, and guilt at eating too much. This went on for a couple of weeks until, trying to find out what was causing it, I remembered that after my birth experience in the seed group, I had a tremendously strong urge to suck. I checked with my mother and found she didn't feed me as soon as I was born – so a possible explanation is that I'd gone back to this infantile experience of wanting to suck and not being able to. It certainly explains a lot – like my thumb sucking in particular and, more generally, my strong and continued dissatisfaction with everything, that nothing is quite right. After all, it was the first thing I ever wanted, and I didn't get it. It seems to me I've been looking for that all my life. Anyway, once I'd realised this and thought about it the obsession for eating just disappeared, and I felt much better straight away.

This situation could have been speeded up by attempting to see where the feelings had been experienced in the past; or by having another session with the question held as to where the continuous urge to eat arose from. Also, the woman was not regularly using coex, so it took her longer to clarify what arose in the one session.

As was said at the beginning of this chapter, coex is a natural process. As such it does not need any techniques or special settings. But like any natural force, such as electricity, different structures cause it to express different qualities. These structures are ones I have found useful. You need to find which is most suitable for yourself.

CHAPTER 3

Opening the Doors of Mind and Body

There is a big difference between knowing about coex intellectually, and being ready and able to experience it. This is partly because coex is very real. Coex is connected with the dream process, and inherent in the experience of that process is:-

A That we are deeply involved in what is produced. It is not simply something we consider at a remove – we are it!

B It is ego-alien. It produces things we have not necessarily created already in our conscious ego. Therefore we have to realise that what we call 'I', the attitudes, beliefs, memories and reactions we associate as being 'us', is only an island in a large sea. It is only a resonably small part of the many biological and psychological activities which together constitute our existence. In a sense it is one small room in a large and complex house. The walls of the room are the boundaries between ourself and the other aspects of our existence. During our waking life we may seldom go beyond those boundaries. Perhaps ours is a square room, and some other people live in round, oblong or triangular rooms. If someone whose boundaries are thus different to ours – we might believe in God and they do not – questions our attitude or views, it might be upsetting, irritating or even frightening. Such fears and irritations make up the walls of the boundaries we place between ourself and 'otherness'. The forces of life in us, our own complete memories, and the sum total of what we compute from our entire experience, might be this very 'other'.

The following description by Ian is an example of this in the action of coex itself. He says:

For some months, in my weekly work with coex, I had been experiencing movements which I felt were improving the health of my body. Many of the movements were unusual, ones which I could never have thought of. They seemed to be acting on parts of my body which felt painful or stiff. For instance for some time before starting coex I had what felt like a grumbling appendix. During my practice some of the movements which arose really massaged that area of my body. Subsequently the discomfort has disappeared. In this way my body was led to greater mobility. Then one week, without prior warning, something new arose. The session started with movements which were like setting up exercises – bending and squatting. A few moments of stillness followed, then suddenly I began to dance. No, that's not quite right – I was danced from within, for I didn't know the plan of the dance. I danced creation. With great sweeping movements I gathered material from the space around me. With mighty breath I blew upon what was being formed, and gradually a world was created. It was a great world which I then carried upon my shoulders like Atlas. But so mighty was this world I gradually fell beneath its weight, crushed and unable to rise. I lay there, trapped, but gradually a feeling arose that there was something within me from which strength could come if I struggled and did not give up. So, like a captive giant I strove against the ponderous weight of my own creation until the deeper strength rose from within me. With difficulty I lifted the world from off my back to my chest. Then gradually I rose. As if it were a ball on the end of a chain I swung the world around me, slowly at first, but then faster and faster. Then suddenly and with great relief I let go and the world was gone. Then I seemed to be standing before a bright and loving light. Although the world was gone, I still felt as if my hands were chained, and as spontaneously as the dance, words rose in me, asking the light to remove them. But the light replied, 'Ian, I have never chained you, only you have bound yourself'. Although I didn't understand in what way I had chained myself, the realisation of it being my own doing caused the chains to drop off and I lifted my hands to the light, bathing in its laughter and love. From a deep part of me a song was called, and I sang to the light my thanks and love. Then came laughter, for I had been such a fool.

Slowly the powerful feelings ebbed away and I was left quiet but amazed at what had flowed through me. Being in some ways a shy person I had never before danced in my life. So to first do stretching exercises, then dance and sing because of the release and love I felt left me almost in a state of wonder. Where had it all come from? What did it mean?

It took almost three months for me to really begin to answer those questions. Then, one day when I was describing the experience to a friend I suddenly realised what it was saying. Before starting coex I had felt very ill, but also ill at ease with myself. At that time, although I had not been brought up in an actively religious family, I had lived by a strong religious code. I dealt with difficulties in my marriage and myself by applying the rigid morals I used to guide my life. I disciplined myself to live the sort of life I felt God called me to live. That was the world I had created. I had made a world so rigid and heavy to bear that it had crushed me and made me ill. Through coex I was beginning to throw off that old way of life and the restrictions I had placed upon myself. I had begun to develop a sense of meeting life face to face, instead of creating a God in the mould of my own narrow conceptions. I had begun to feel a communication with life itself within me, and truly it way saying – 'Ian, I have never chained you.'

What Ian describes shows how he found something which was outside and more complete than his usual personality. It has in it many of the conditions Freud stated as being relevant to dreams. So not only is Ian's experience of coex apparently connected with the process underlying dreams, but it is more healing than most dreams, and enlarges his realm of experience. He found these things because he could allow the otherness that was himself to enter his waking life. So the recognition that coex will require us to allow other possibilities, other experiences, viewpoints and emotions than we usually allow ourselves, is basic. Also, this 'allowing' really means that we are letting ourselves experience things very fully, not just intellectually, but as one does in a dream, with personal involvement.

The illness Ian mentions was pain in the chest, tiredness and depression. The chest pain was diagnosed as psychosomatic by his doctor, but was nevertheless a very real pain. This, his tiredness and depression gradually disappeared as he used the process of coex. But this only occurred because he took something to the process. What he took was regular practice over a period of years. Although there were highlights in what he experienced, as described above, there was only a gradual change to health in himself. Also he took agreement and his consent. Not only did he consent to the action of coex by continuing it, but when he was confronted by possible changes in his view of life as in his dance, when he realised what the dance meant, he agreed to take a chance on those changes suiting him. He did this by surrendering something of the rigid views by which he had previously lived. So, some degree of preseverance, agreement and surrender are necessary attitudes we need in the use of coex.

If we remember that we are dealing with the dream process, and this process can create a spontaneous drama which can involve our whole being, then in the practice itself we need to 'hang loose'. So apart from attitudes, the first step of practice is to learn a form of relaxation in which our body has dropped unecessary tension, and is like a keyboard ready to be played. I find it helps if we create something of this feeling consciously, holding our body, our emotions, our sexuality, mind and memories as if they were keys upon which the inner dramatist can play. In a sense we are seeking to create a condition similar to sleep. As we fall asleep we let go of our control over what we think, what we do with our body, and what we fantisise. Our 'I', our decision making self has relaxed and left the stage free for the dream maker to create its realisations. So in approaching coex we need to take on a similar relaxed state without actually going to sleep. Dreams are not as healing as coex, mostly because we do not consciously cooperate and agree with the process. It, therefore, does not integrate as fully with our waking self.

Many people can easily hang loose, and so coex occurs freely. But in case this is not so, there are some things we can do to learn it. These are tools we can use which can help us define what it feels like to allow our body and mind to be loose enough for spontaneous expression. As such they need not be used once that is learnt.

1 This is a simple and enjoyable technique which gives a direct experience of spontaneous movement. You need to stand about a foot away from a wall, side on. Start with your right side. You are going to lift your right arm sideways, but because you are near the wall you will only manage to lift it part of the way. So when the back of your hand touches the wall, press it hard against the wall as if trying to complete the movement of lifting the arm. Using a reasonable amount of effort stay with the hand pressing against the wall for about thirty seconds. Then move so you face away from the wall, and with eyes closed relax your arm and be aware of what happens. Try it before reading on, and use the left arm afterwards.

What we have done is to attempt to make a movement. Because the wall prevented this, the body was not able to complete the movement you asked it to make. Therefore a muscular charge built up in the deltoid muscle. When you stepped away from the wall the arm, if relaxed, was then free to complete the movement. So possibly your arm rose from your side as if weightless, thus discharging its energy. Some people need several tries before they can find the right body feeling to allow the arm its movement. It is easy to prevent it moving because the impulse is quite a subtle one. The point of the exercise however, is to learn a relationship with oneself in which the subtle impulse can express. The movement the arm makes, and how it feels to experience an unwilled movement, is so similar to coex we are thus provided with an experimental experience of the real thing. Therefore it is helpful either to practice the technique until you can do it, or use it a number of times to establish your relationship with the feeling of it. This sense of allowing movement can then be used in coex itself.

2 For the next technique you need to work with a partner. One person needs to be the subject' and the other the 'helper'. The subject can stand or lay down, and the helper should take their hands. The subject should close their eyes and be in a 'hang loose' feeling. The helper should give the subject a few moments to feel relaxed in the situation, then start slowly moving their arms in random movements. If there is noticeable tension or resistance to their arms being moved, the helper should attempt to help the subject be aware of such tensions or points of resistance. Sometimes the arms are so tense they will stay in any position they are placed. Then it is easy enough to point out to the subject how they are tensing their arms. Otherwise, perhaps the helper can manage to have the subject feel the areas where resistance occurs, and have them learn to go along with the movements with less effort. This is the aim of this technique. One is helping the subject feel what it is like to have their body moved by someone/something other than their own directions. As this is a learning process, this may need some practice.

In some cases it will be noticed if you are the helper, that the subject is trying to help you make the movements of the arms. If so, while still moving their arms in a random way, gradually lessen your direction and let them take the lead. If you do this slowly the person will feel you are still directing the movements of their arms. As this point is reached, take your hands away gently and encourage the subject to let their hands and arms explore their own movements. This is a gentle and effective way for some people to be led into the experience of coex. Once they are making their own movements, with the attitude that 'you' are doing it, they have effectively learnt how to allow spontaneous fantasy to take place.

In her article on coex which appeared in Harpers and Queen, Leslie Kenton describes a woman's experience who was led into coex by the above method. She says:

> I watched one woman, who was using the technique for the first time, lie quietly breathing. She then found that her hands began to move gently as though she was exploring the texture and quality of space near her body. Crisp encouraged her to go with these fine movements. Gradually they developed into larger stroking gestures in the air around her. Her imaging facilities came into

play as the physical movements continued and she sensed that she was in what she later described as a kind of womb. But instead of being dark it was permeated with light, immensely safe and beautiful. Then gradually her torso and shoulders began to move as well until slowly she emerged from this extraordinary womb world into clear air and more light. She began to weep quietly, stunned by the power and the beauty of an experience which had come quite spontaneously from within her. When she later began to try and make sense of the imagery which accompanied the movements she realised that her own feeling sense [which until then she had not even been aware of] had created for her a physical expression of the particular life situation she was in at the moment. She was on the verge of a new beginning as far as her work was concerned, and had been feeling rather unsettled and anxious about it. She found this coex experience enormously helpful because it made her realise that the career changes she had planned had not been motivated by some capricious wish but were very much in line with the direction her deepest self was leading her. She also discovered that she has a feeling sense which she can experience for herself and that if she listens to it, it will express a summary of her life situation at any particular time or help her work through whatever blocks or tensions she experiences.

Movements of Meaning

As already explained, our mind or feeling self is linked with our body through movement. It is sometimes clearer for us to observe this in other animals than in ourselves. The expression of sexual drive, for instance, and the follow up of parenting, can easily be seen as physical movements of an instinctive nature in the elaborate courtship rituals of some birds. The movements of these rituals, and the movements of nest making, are examples of spontaneously generated activity. If such movements were inhibited for some reason, the animal would undoubtedly experience physical tension and internal stress. A puppy I once owned demonstrated this to me after I had trained her to sit and wait while I put her food in her bowl. Her instinctive drive was to move to engulf the food. I had put an artificial block to that impulse by smacking her each time she did it. The result was that while she waited from me to give her permission to eat, her body exhibited enormous trembling. As soon as my block was removed and she could allow her movements, the trembling ceased.

A dog can express its natural and impulsive drives to eat, to chase, bark, be aggressive and have sex more openly than most human beings. Because of our social training we have often built into ourselves quite enormous physical tensions to hold back our feelings and the movements which would express them. The action of coex is a means of releasing the tensions by allowing the body and feelings to express themselves in a 'safe' environment without inhibition. But coex itself cannot function sometimes because the very tensions it would release are inhibiting its action. Therefore it is often helpful to begin releasing such tensions in another more structured way. This can be done by making some of the movements we might have made if the body were freely expressing itself. Note has been taken of typical movements different people make during coex, and these have been put together in a series of exercises. While these are only necessary prior to coex if we have difficulty in starting, they are pleasureable to do, and probably better for health than general physical movements. This is because each one expresses in some way an inner function such as sex, extroversion, introversion, taking, giving, etc. They therefore integrate body and mind more fully than a simple keep-fit exercise. Originally all movement was linked with a function or meaningful activity such as hunting, communicating, and so on. While these movements are not as powerful as either those directly expressing our needs, or those arising in coex, they are extremely helpful.

1 This first movement we start from a standing position. With feet slightly apart we take an in-breath, and as we reach the high point of inhalation we take head and arms backwards to really open up the chest. From that standing position with head back you then begin to breath out and bend the knees so that you can drop quickly into a squat. As you do so let the arms move forward and up so the hands come palms together near to the face. Meanwhile you drop into a squatting position expelling your breath fast as you go down. You rest there for a moment and then the movement carries on by breathing in and rising back up to the first position again. So you slowly stand as you breath in, then when standing expand the rib cage again by opening the arms slightly backwards and apart, and taking the head slightly back.

The going down into the squatting position should be done fairly fast with the outbreath quite strong so that there is a WHHHHH, an audible blowing of air out of the lungs. It can be done gently, but if possible, do it strongly as the body drops. Let the hips go down as far as you comfortably can, and let the head collapse down too so the body is relaxed. Some people need to put their heels on books to make squatting comfortable, so do that if necessary. The hands come forward in a scything movement until they meet just above the dropped head.

The movement expresses in postures the two basic ways we deal with our energy – by exteriorising it, or interiorising it. The down position is introversion, and the up an extroversion. It is helpful to get something of the feeling of this as you do the movement. The exercise needs to be done for about a minute, and the aim of it is to get the body systems working, such as breathing and circulation. But also it needs to be done over a period of time, as with the others, until it can be felt as a flowing expressive movement without kinks and blocks. As we are using the movements to help release tensions, they should be done even in the face of feeling very awkward or incapable of them. Such are the feelings tensions produce to resist our removal of them. After the exercise is done, sit or stand for a minute and simply 'imagine' that you are doing the movement. See if you can repeat within yourself the different feelings states – of being 'up' and 'down' – that occurred while actually doing the exercise. If you cannot remember those feelings, do the movement to remind yourself.

2 The next movement you begin in the same position as the first, but feet slightly further apart, about shoulder width. Then, keeping your head and shoulders more or less floating in the same position, circle the hips. The hips are taken gradually into a wide circle; so, as the hips are circling back the trunk is slightly bent forward, but still with the head high. The hips should go well out to the side, and as they swing to the front, they should be far forward enough to cause the trunk to be inclined slightly backwards. If you cannot manage this at first, simply do what you can. The knees and ankles should be kept relaxed, as should the hips themselves, so they adapt to the circling. As the hips rotate, if the pelvis is reasonably relaxed, it swings backwards and forwards with the movement. Do not make the movement complicated by attempting to reproduce these finer points, they will come as your body loosens and the tensions melt. The breathing should then also find its own rhythm. Generally it is out as the hips swing forward, and in as they swing backwards. This is because the chest is slightly compressed as the hips are forward, that is, if the head is floating erect.

The movement needs to be done for about a minute, and at half time rotate the hips in the opposite direction from which you started. The first movement expressed a mobility of energy and so does this – the circulation of energy within us.

So after the movement is finished, stand or sit, and reproduce the feelings of the exercise without moving your body.

3 This movement is the most important single exercise in the series. Still in the standing position, with the feet about six inches apart, this time we are swinging our pelvis backwards and forwards while rotating the hips from back to front. This may need some practice, so if you stand and imagine you are taking your hips backward to hollow the lower back and then swing them forward, that is the basis of the movement. As the pelvis swings backwards it hollows the lower back, and when forward it causes the chest/rib cage to slightly collapse.

If you try, and find you can do that, it now needs to be developed into a wider movement. So I will describe the whole movement from the beginning carefully. From a standing position you tilt the hips backwards. hollowing the lower back, and continue this backward tilt as if you were going to sit down in a chair, allowing the knees to bend slightly to keep your balance. Although it is necessary to describe this in sections, the movement needs to be a flowing one. But in this position the trunk is slightly forwards, the breath in and the rib cage expanded. At the end of the backwards swing let the hips begin to push forwards. At the same time begin to straighten the legs and breathe out. What this does is bring the hips in a circling movement from back to front. Because the knees were bent as the hips went back, the circle is down and back, forwards and up, until you return to the standing position from which you started and continue the movement.

Not only does the pelvis swing backwards and forwards in the movement, the legs bend and straighten, the chest is expanded and collapsed, and as you gain fluidity, a wave of movement runs up the spine. If the chest is kept rigid this will not happen. So the chest and neck need to kept loose and ready to respond to the hip movements.

Sex in animals is expressed as spontaneous movements. In human beings the hips are often so immobile it is impossible for this spontaneity to occur. But this exercise is much more than something to mobilise our sexual responsiveness. Because the spine is the main nerve trunk for our whole body, and because movement is life [i.e. the big difference between a dead and a live body is that the live one moves] the spinal waves created in the movement help the whole body to come alive in the sense of releasing energy from tensions and in mobility and expressive movement. Also, this movement, together with the one before it and the next one, are extremely helpful in easing or removing lower back pains caused by tension or back strain.

This exercise expresses the giving and receiving, the yes and no of relationships. When you finish it, sit or stand and recreate the feelings of it by imagining the movement. You may find your breathing responds to what you are imagining. This is normal.

4 This exercise can be called 'roller skating'. You stand with feet a little wider than shoulder width and with the trunk bent forward and knees bent as well. The back should be reasonably straight although at an incline. You now swing the hips from side to side. If possible let most of the movement occur from below the navel. You can keep you eyes looking ahead, your arms swinging in time with the hips to let the body move fully. But it is the lower back which is being worked here, although the movement massages the lower internal organs as well, so you may get a stitch until you adapt to the exercise. Do the movement fairly vigorously. If you do get a stitch, do not stop altogether, just slow down. The movement will then massage the area of discomfort. After you have finished the exercise, imagine you are making the movements to recreate the feeling of it.

5 In this exercise we need to stand with the feet as wide as we comfortably can. Be careful to check how slippery your feet are on the floor surface. If they are too slippery to easily maintain a feet-wide position, it may help to take your stockings/socks off. From this position let your trunk drop and the arms to droop forward, allowing the spine to be gently stretched. When you feel your spine has adapted to the position, from an outbreath swing your spine and head to the left, allowing it to roll over and up to the standing position as you breathe in. You drop the trunk downwards in the middle again breathing out – do it fairly fast – then roll head and trunk to the right as you come up and breathe in again. The movement is an active one, with a light pause as you reach top and bottom. Some people like to allow their arms to extend in a wide arc as they come up. It feels more balanced. Also, as you come to the upright position with the inbreath, let the head drop back slightly, and arms extend sideways and back to increase the chest stretch. This balances the deep exhalation accomplished by dropping the trunk forward.

This is a very pleasing movement, and because it connects with the breath cycle, develops a particular rhythm. If you can manage it without becoming giddy, let the exhaling of breath as you go down be quite energetic. When the exercise is finished, imagine doing it while sitting or standing. Psychologically, this movement expresses energy up and down the spine. But it also has an element of bowing before something, then standing energetically erect.

6 This movement works the abdominal muscles quite

strongly, and needs to be approached slowly until you feel confident and able in it. It is not primarily a physical exercise. It is an expression of letting go of self, of surrendering. You start with feet about shoulder width apart. From an inbreath you drop your head slowly back and breathe out, allowing your head, shoulders and trunk to drop slightly backwards with the arms limp. If you are comfortable in that, allow your trunk to drop backwards while you breathe as you can. The point of the movement is not to see how far backward you can go. It is to express the feeling of letting go of self, of dropping control in a disciplined way. This comes about because the top of the body is surrendered, but the lower part is highly organised to support that surrender. This is very much what coex is. So the dropping backwards need only be very slight unless your spine is flexible.

When the head and shoulders are back, at first hold the position for a very short time, then recover to the upright stance. As you get used to the movement, you can stay in the surrendered position longer – just as long as is comfortable – then recover. The meditation of this movement is to create the sense of letting go, of surrender, without moving the body much. In this way we can create this feeling in ourselves when we come to use coex and need to let go of our muscular and emotional control. It is also important to recognise and create the feeling of recovery to the erect, self directing stance. Coex is partly a way of learning how to direct the processes of our being more capably, and these two stances are important.

7 This exercise uses the legs a lot more, and introduces more spinal twist. You start with feet about a metre apart in a standing position, and with the hands palms together in front of the chest. Turn the left foot to point to the left, and as you turn the trunk to face in that direction, let the left knee bend until the hips drop right down near the left heel. To make this easier, let the left heel rise. In other words, do not try to keep the foot flat on the floor. Meanwhile the right leg is trailing right out behind you, forming an arc up from the floor along the spine. The right knee is on the floor but hardly bent.

As this lunge to the left occurs, from the hands together

position, let the right hand reach forward in the direction you are lunging, and the left arm stretch out backward toward the right foot – i.e. in the same direction. This gives a slight spinal twist, although the head should be facing front. Also, although you are reaching forwards with the right hand, there is a common tendency for people to extend the whole trunk forward too, and that is unnecessary. The trunk curves upright from the trailing leg.

From the lunge position, using the strength of the left leg push back towards the upright position, bringing the hands back to be centred in front of the chest again. The breathing sequence for this being out as you lunge, in as you centre again. Then from the centred position you lunge to the right. Do not forget that it is now the left arm you extend forwards – always the opposite hand. Pause in the lunge then using the strength of the right leg push up and centre again.

I find this movement one of the most enjoyable, and there is a way of doing it which makes it flowing and a unity between breathing, moving and meditaion. But before that can be done, you need to practice the exercise until you can do it without too much thought. Then, do the movement slowly, as if it were an expression of the breath being unhurriedly expelled as you lunge. Hold the position for a pause, then slowly back on the inhale, once again pausing. The exhalation should be felt inwardly as a giving out of oneself, and the inhalation as a receiving. As you can probably now begin to see, the movements are thus expressing some of the basic energy/feeling states – introversion/extroversion; surrender/control; giving/receiving; relaxed/dynamic. So not only are the series designed to mobilise our bodies by taking them through their possible basic movements, they also mobilise our energy and feelings by calling on them to stretch and move. The still meditation of this exercise is a little more complex than the others, because of the complex body patterns, but try it while you sit or stand.

8 This movement is a spinal twist, more so than the last. You start by standing with the feet a little wider than shoulder width and with the hands at the sides. Leading with the head, we turn to the left, letting your arms describe a wide circle, and continuing their movement when head and trunk can turn no further. As the trunk turns to the left, let the feet and knees accommodate the twist, so that when you have turned as far as you can to the left, your left knee is lightly bent in a lunge to allow the fullest turn. Now turn from there to the right, going round as far as you can, fairly slow to let the feet and legs change. The arms are extended describing a wide arc, and coming to rest where you feel comfortable, but not floppy. The breath cycle is to complete exhalation as the spinal twist is complete, and to complete inhalation as you reach mid-point between the left and right twist. Like the previous exercise, if the breathing is united with the movement, it makes for a more satisfying experience. Once you have got the feel for integrating breathing and movement, perform this one fairly slowly and purposefully. End by imaging this one while sitting or standing in stillness.

9 This exercise is very difficult to describe in a book, but as it is important an attempt will be made to make it clear. It is a standing movement which aims at mobilising the rib cage in one of its movements we seldom make in everyday life. Keeping the hips still, it is possible for the lower ribs to swing slightly sideways. If we do this with the right side of the rib-case, it causes the left shoulder to drop, and the right to rise. When we alternately extend the right and left sides of the lower rib-case, the shoulders alternately rise and fall as well. Therefore, if one lifts and drops the shoulders alternately, this may help produce the extending of the rib-case, but not necessarily so. Many people move their shoulders in this way, or swing their hips energetically, without their rib-case being mobilised at all. As the chest in general is highly expressive of emotions, as seen in crying and laughing, any such inability to move the rib-case suggests tensions or repressed emotions in the area.

To make sure your movement is actually doing what it should, it is helpful at first to practice in front of a mirror. Keeping the hips still and rib-case centred, hold your index fingers about two inches away from each side of your lower ribs. Now see if you can swing the ribs sideways towards the extended but still finger without swaying the whole trunk and hips sideways as well. At first you may not know just what muscles to move to accomplish this, but with practise it becomes simple. Like one of the earlier movements, this one may cause you to develop a 'stitch' if you do it fairly actively. This is because it strongly massages the internal organs, which is a healthful stimulus to them. It may also cause an unusual bellows action with the lungs, causing a pumping of air in and out of the lungs without actually breathing. This is quite normal for the movement, and is not harmful. The movement should be ended by the still meditation.

10 In a general sense we have been moving up the body in this series of exercises, and so are concentrating more on the chest and shoulders at the moment. This exercise is primarily to mobilise the shoulders and rib-case in relationship to the spine. But it also brings the arms into action in more than the supporting role so far encountered. Start by standing with feet about shoulder width apart. Be aware of the knees, and keep them very slightly bent and relaxed. Keeping your head and hips still, bring the hands up to the breasts and take the elbows backwards and close to the trunk. Now, keeping the left elbow back, reach forward with the right hand until the right shoulder swings forward a little, and the left elbow pulls back a bit more. Meanwhile, the head and hips should remain facing forward, so that the shoulders swing around the steady spine. Now swing the left hand forward and the right back, bring the right elbow back and down as the left was. Then alternate the arms reaching and pulling back. The movement can be done slowly but strongly, or fast and energetically.

This exercise expresses giving and taking, like the lunge, but more forcefully. If you feel any aggression in the movement, let it be expressed. Like the last movement, this too may cause air to be pumped in and out of the lungs. Finish with the still meditation of the movement.

11 This is more of a meditation than an exercise, but is important in mobilising inner feelings which lay behind movements. Stand in a comfortable balanced position with the hands in front of the chest, palms together and eyes closed. Imagine that as you breathe in the air is fanning a small glowing coal inside the chest. The incoming air makes the coal glow gently, and you breathe slowly and with awareness. This coal is just a symbol of the subtle pleasure sensations generated by slow purposeful inhalation. If you can be directly aware of this pleasure, dispense with the image of the coal. In either case, let the hands indicate the amount of this glow or pleasure. Let them do this by moving apart, so that if the pleasure is intense the hands reach wide. As you exhale and the glow fades, let the hands come together. But if there is little felt, then the hands remain unopened. When you begin this meditation, do not be in a hurry to open the hands to let the feeling of pleasure radiate out. In fact, let the hands be as spontaneous in expressing what you feel as you can. In consequence it may be that your hands move a great deal, or very little. At the end of this moving meditation, there is no need to repeat it as a still meditation.

12 These exercises, and the meditations accompanying them, may have introduced you to the idea of mobilising ones internal energy flow and ones attitudes or feelings as well as releasing tension and stiffness in the body. Yet physical tension is only partly to do with not flexing ones limbs and spine enough. Such terms as stiffnecked, heavy handed, rigid, and no backbone, although apparently referring to the body are actually describing character traits. Even if such character traits do not cause physical stiffness, to live with them is perhaps even worse than not being able to touch ones toes or turn ones head. A great deal of bloodshed in the world arises out of people living in such narrow political or religious beliefs that they are ready to kill others who do not share them. That may be an extreme, but most of us have some areas of stiffness or pain in our soul. This is mentioned because this exercise, although completely physical, confronts many people with either the narrowness of some of their attitudes or the stiffness of their feelings.

In this exercise we explore the use of sound. To make different sounds we need to move not only our throat, but also our trunk and even limbs in different ways. Sounds also evoke feelings and move or exercise them. Just as many of us do not move our bodies outside certain restricted and habitual gestures and actions, so also our range of sounds may be quite small. So for several minutes explore making sounds. Start by taking a full breath and letting it out noisily with an AHHHH sound. Do this until you feel it resonating in your body and change to a strong EEEEEEEEEEE sound. Then try MMMMMMMAAAAAA.

If you are doing this exercise for the first time, that is sufficient for one session. As your sound production improves though, and you begin to enjoy it, explore making all sorts of happy sounds; different sorts of laughter, proud, childish, funny, etc; angry noises; animal and bird noises; sensual sounds; the sound of crying or sobbing; natural sounds such as wind, water, earthquakes; make the sounds of different languages and different situations such as a warriors chant, a mothers lullaby (without real words, just evocative sounds), a lover's song, a hymn to Life, or even sounds about birth and death; and just plain nonsense noises. Do not attempt to explore all these different types of sound at one session. Just choose one and explore it until you can feel yourself limbering up in it and getting past restricting feelings such as shyness or stupidness. Those are the walls of restriction.

Because the above exercises are excellent preparation, coex can be practised directly after them. I am not suggesting they should always precede coex, simply that having done the movements the use of coex is an excellent finish. If used in this way, a period of rest or relaxation at the end of coex would be useful.

The Sense of Nonsense

In an unpublished manuscript I was fortunate enough to be loaned, Dr. Caron Kent describes how some of his patients found healing through working with the self-regulatory forces in themselves. More interesting still in regard to what we are considering here, he also describes how he first made contact with the process of coex in himself. He says that he had been feeling unwell for some time, and as a doctor recognised his condition was more psychological than physical. He felt he needed to discover the latent resources of his own being and so decided to regularly give time to be with himself and learn. He did this by sitting at his typewriter and writing whatever came into his feelings or thoughts. At first such writings were disjointed, meaningless and appeared to be of no help to him. But he persisted, and into his spontaneous writing began to emerge pieces of information and insights into his nature which started the process of change and healing. He later refined his technique and used it to help others, as described in his book THE PUZZLED BODY – Vision Press.

Although this differs from Jung's approach in techniques used, nevertheless the underlying principle is exactly the same. Jung suggests fantasising with the hands, Caron Kent used his typewriter. People have used an enormous variety of approaches to experience coex, but basically what underlies each is that they have trusted their own nature and dared to allow seemingly irrational parts of themselves expression. Their belief in the resources of their own being was a powerful demand directed to their inner process to produce something helpful. Continuance in the face of initial meaninglessness made their demand an organising and disciplining force to draw sense out of the original jumbled expression of their unconscious. Whether we are attempting to define a new and more useful view of the world, to ease aches in our soul, or to transcend the limitations we find in our art or love, some aims in our life are big enough to need persistence in the face of obstacles.

We can consider our bodies, with their variety of faculties, as our typewriter, or equipment extraordinary. I know that people may already have defined a working relationship with coex through their activity in such things as painting, music, dancing, etc. Nevertheless I still believe it is worthwhile learning to relate to coex directly through ourself. This need not in any way detract from other techniques we use. In fact I believe it can only add to them, for they are all extensions of our basic bodily and psychological functions. Also, this direct approach links with some of the ways our internal processes work.

Although it has already been quoted in an earlier book, it helps to be clear about this point of allowing physical fantasy if one understands the way completely unconscious inner events gradually emerge into consciousness. M.V. Caldwell, writing about the way Van Rhijn has defined the levels of consciousness says there are four stages:–

1 The deeply unconscious physiological process, such as cell generation and digestion. Problems which cannot move more fully into consciousness and so are held at this level, become psychosomatic pains or illness. This becomes clearer if we consider human life in relationship with other life forms. A plant for instance might have some sort of bacterial illness, but would not be able to bring that to awareness. In a sense many things which occur to us, although they are very real and definite, never become a part of our conscious life, but always remain in the 'plant' level. If they are to move from 'deeply unconscious physiological process' to becoming known consciously, there are stages such events go through.

2 As the physiological or psychobiological process moves nearer consciousness, its next level of expression is postural or gestural. Thus we may express our deepest hidden feelings in an unconscious body posture or movement. Not only our feelings express themselves in this way, but also our physical tone or health shows in our gestures and movements. Even the plant droops if it needs water.

3 Next, when something moves from the gestural to the next stage of expression it becomes a dream or a symbol, which although it may not be understood, is now entering the arena of awareness.

4 At this stage, what had been deeply unconscious, then symbolised, now becomes known enough to be verbalised or thought about and analysed. If one had attempted to verbalise something in level two it would have been so far outside consciousness as to defy description. Also, when looking at these levels or stages, they suggest that the dream process is a means by which deeper stages can be portrayed to awareness in order to make them known. Therefore, by working with the dream process via coex, we can tap deeper levels of awareness and make them known.

An interesting example of these four stages and how someone can work through them is given by Reich. When the abdominal tensions of a patient were released the man found his body making spontaneous movements. These were allowed and the movements gradually led the man to take on the posture of an animal – he and Reich both felt it to be a fish. This puzzled both of them as to its meaning, but as the movements continued the man first realised he felt like a fish caught on a hook and line, then suddenly, that was how he felt in regard to his mother.

As can be plainly seen, the first level is seen in the example as the mans unconscious abdominal tensions, built into his physical structure. When these are loosened and considered by the mans conscious attention, and the spontaneous self-regulatory/dream process is allowed to function, level two manifests as movement and gesture. This moves to level three where the movements are recognised as a symbol – the fish. Then the fourth level, insight and understanding are achieved when the man realises the fish represents previously unconscious feelings he has about his mother. At this point he can verbalise and analyse. I believe that being aware of such facts enables us more easily to open ourselves to the process of self-regulation and trust what it produces.

Giving the Urge to Health the Right Setting

Apart from this mental setting, the physical and emotional environment we choose to practice in is important too. When I had been seeking coex for some time, my very first experience of it came while I was sitting in a local church relaxing. As I dropped tension my head began to be pulled backwards in spontaneous movement. I was excited by this and attempted to allow what was happening to take its course. Even so the movement disappeared within moments. Much later in the company of friends interested in coex, and in a room we were using for its practice, the movement appeared again. This time it continued and was fully released in a re-enactment of having my tonsils out.

The setting and its social and emotional environment are extremely important. The movements and sound I experienced in re-enacting my tonsil operation would have been highly unacceptable and difficult to explain in the setting of a country church. In the company of my friends however, I could relax and know that whatever was produced in my practice would be sympathetically assessed. Setting, therefore, includes more than simply the room we use or the friends we keep. This is brought out clearly by the experience of Joy whose doctor diagnosed a muscular illness because of spasms in her arm muscles. She had lived under the shadow of this 'illness' for some years before she attended a coex group and saw that such spasms were a natural attempt on the part of her self-regulatory process to release tension.

The aspect of setting that Joy confronted is of course an integral part of our own nature in some degree. As already said, an easy relationship with the unconscious is not something our culture teaches or encourages. Therefore, in teaching people how to learn the process I have been asked certain questions over and over again. People ask: "Is it dangerous? If I let go of the hold I have on my emotions, will I lose control or go mad?" . . . "Is this against my religion? When I leave myself open like this, will evil forces take hold of me?" . . . "Isn't it bad to express your negative emotions? Surely it's healthier to keep them in myself and not load them onto other people."

Because such ideas and feelings can stand in the way of allowing ones own urge to health a reasonable area of expression, they need careful thought. Although I am going to look at each of the questions, it is important that if you find these questions in yourself you need to take them seriously. They are standards you have been living by. As such you are using them now to assess the safety or usefulness of something new. Such standards may have been given to you ready formed by your family, your culture, or a group you belong to. Any such standards which you accept as valid will decide the directions you choose in life. Therefore you need to check them thoroughly to see if they are based on anxiety or observable facts.

Coex Code of Practice

IS IT DANGEROUS – WILL I GO MAD...There are dangers attached to any undertaking. Most of us drive a car or ride in motorised transport despite the fact that tens of thousands of human beings die annually in such transport. But when we learn to drive a car we recognise that the dangers attached to it are lessened by learning certain rules applying to it, such as driving on a particular side of the road. In the use of coex it is largely a natural process which has its own built-in safety factors. Nevertheless there are certain things which are important to its use – rules of the road so to speak. These are as follows:–

1 If you have any history of being hospitalized for mental illness you should not practice coex. Jung sums this up when he writes, "In this way (by letting things happen), a new attitude is created, an attitude which accepts the irrational and the unbelievable, simply because it is what is happening. THIS ATTITUDE WOULD BE POISON FOR A PERSON WHO HAS ALREADY BEEN OVERWHELMED BY THINGS THAT JUST HAPPEN..."

2 Because one is dealing with the dream process, some of what arises will be in symbolic form. Such symbols, whether in the form of the danced story or feeling oneself like an animal, need to be gently enquired into. They need to be understood in reference to ones everyday life, as did the man who acted out being a fish. If this is not done a degree of unclarity or lack of integration will occur. In terms of the four stages of consciousness, our symbol level has not unified with our verbal intellectual self.

Despite having observed hundreds of people use coex I have not seen anyone 'go mad'. I have seen one woman who had an undeclared history of hospitalization for a manic condition – in which she flew so high into feelings of idealism and what she called love, that all practical issues such as the care of her child were forgotten – again enter those feelings and need the help of tablets to bring her down to earth once more. In her case coex had not caused her condition, it had only triggered it into operation again, as did other events in her life.

What coex often does do though, is to bring people to a

completely new and more relaxed relationship with their unconscious. People who had been afraid of their unconscious rising up and swallowing them in 'madness' learnt to meet it as a friend and ally. The irrational was seen not to be something crazy to guard against like an enemy within, but as a natural part of ones own being, also working for ones survival. A patient of Jung's sent him the following letter describing her own feelings about this:

> Out of evil much good has come to me. By keeping quiet, repressing nothing, remaining attentive, and hand in hand with that, by accepting reality – taking things as they are, and not as I wanted them to be – by doing all this, rare knowledge has come to me, and rare powers as well, such as I could never have imagined before. I always thought that when we accept things, they overpower us in some way or another. Now this is not true at all, and it is only by accepting them that one can define an attitude toward them. So now I intend playing the game of life, being receptive to whatever comes to me, good and bad, sun and shadow that are forever shifting, and, in this way, also accepting my own nature with its positive and negative sides. Thus everything becomes more alive to me. What a fool I was! How I tried to force everything to go according to my idea!

IS IT AGAINST MY RELIGION . . . Commenting on the womans letter above, Jung writes:

> We must never forget our historical premises. Only a little more than a thousand years ago we stumbled from the crudest beginnings of ploytheism into the midst of a highly developed, oriental religion which lifted the imaginative minds of half-savages to a height which did not correspond to their degree of mental development. In order to keep to this height in some fashion or other, it was unavoidable that the sphere of the instincts should be thoroughly repressed. Therefore, religious practice and morality took on an outspokenly brutal, almost malicious, character. The repressed elements are naturally not developed, but vegetate further in the unconscious and in their original barbarism . . . Only on

the basis of such an attitude (as the womans acceptance of both sides of herself), which renounces nothing of the values won in the course of Christian development, but which, on the contrary, tries with Christian forbearance to accept the humblest things in oneself, will a higher level of consciousness and culture be possible. This attitude is religious in the truest sense, and therefore therapeutic, for all religions are therapies for the sorrows and disorders of the soul.

SHOULD I KEEP MY NEGATIVE FEELINGS IN...Recent findings in regard to repressed emotions of grief or shock show how by holding back such emotions they can lead to serious illness such as cancer. Even ailments such as the common cold, which were once thought to be the result only of exposure to germs, are now known to also afflict us when our immune system is weakened by stress. When investigating why some people come through a period of stress such as bereavement in good health, and others develop serious illness, Dr. Peter Knapp, professor of psychiatry at Boston University School of Medicine, came to the conclusion that, "The ones who stay healthy actively grieve. They think about what's happened to them and gradually work it through. If you lock feelings away, it seems as if your body mourns for you by becoming sick."

I have met people who are convinced that if they express such feelings as anger, these negative emotions spread out into the world like an infection, and enter other peoples lives. Obviously, anything we express in word or deed in front of other people can influence them in some way. But what is usually overlooked is that repressed feelings are unconsciously influencing the way we deal with people anyway. I remember a young woman who used coex for the first time and expressed a lot of body movements and angry sounds. Afterwards she told me she had experienced the release of a lot of anger toward her younger sister. She then said, "I never understood before why I could never get close to my sister. Now it is so clear. I was so full of hidden anger I could never feel affection." So coex practiced in the right setting offers a safe and socially acceptable way of releasing emotions which can cause illness or difficult relationships if held inside.

Will Coex Cure All My Ills

One should not think of using coex to replace the necessary skills of doctor, surgeon, psychiatrist or priest. It is a skill or tool we can use to enhance our life. Like any tool its uses are fairly specialised. A hammer is of no use in putting a screw in properly. Coex is useful mostly for people who already deal with their life reasonably successfully, but have particular tensions which need release, or who seek to further their creative ability and have a deeper experience of themselves. People who find it difficult to take responsibility for their own health in some degree, or find it foreign to think of their own life as something which can be improved and renovated like a house, need another approach. Taking these things into account, seeing it as a means of self help rather than a force outside oneself, coex has a place in society. Thousands of people feel an urge to transcend their present life situation. Doctors and therapists have neither the time nor the technique to deal with thousands of people at a time. Yet our present social climate screams out for forces of regeneration and positive change. If we cannot find means by which each person can take up this work themselves, using their own initiative and skill in connection with their own natural resources, then the future looks bleak. If we depend only on professional bodies and individuals, our turn may never come.

Often there is no ready-made answer to what we feel a need for in our lives, we have to wrestle it out with ourselves, sculpt it out of our own natures. Perhaps others can support us in this, but it is still our work, our journey. Similarly, the answer to our world tension is still in the forming – and it is we who are forming it. For myself I often wonder how Faraday felt as he watched the laws of electricity reveal themselves in his experiments. What was in the heart of Stephenson when he was able to demonstrate the laws of steam? I believe that each of us, as we watch the unfolding of one of the great forces of nature at work in us share something as fundamental and life changing as the discovery of magnetism or steam. Magnets in their everyday use now give us direction in the compass, electricity in the dynamo and sound in the loudspeaker. What – explored, researched and used – will this law of human potential breaking into consciousness lead to?

CHAPTER 4

Creative and Healing Facets of Coex

Apart from using coex for general purposes we can approach it with a specific situation. Maria, a woman in her sixties wanted to learn coex because she was experiencing arthritic type pains in her arms and hands. She also frequently felt depressed and seldom went out of her house. She was married, with a retired husband and children living independently. They had a very nice cottage with a garden in a country village. So Maria's home and surroundings were not stressful, and apart from her pains and depression she was still healthy and good looking.

From a physical point of view Maria was somewhat withdrawn. She seldom went out and was cautious in the way she expressed herself in her movements. She was shown how to allow spontaneous movements with her arms, something which she had never even considered before. At first she was hesitant and shy about making such movements in front of her tutor, but persisted. By the third session her movements were vigorous and began to include her whole body. At that point she stated that quite strong inner feelings of sensual pleasure, even sexuality accompanied the movements she made. This disturbed her a little, but when she had talked it over with her tutor she could accept them as her own healthy feelings being allowed to express themselves. Over the following two weeks a rapid change occured in her. She started going out again and enjoyed it. She bought herself a new outfit of clothes, and the pains in her arms disappeared. At the end of six sessions Maria said she no longer needed further appointments, she had found the change in herself which she had sought.

It seems likely that Maria had been negating her own

healthy flow of pleasure and energy, and it had become depressed instead of expressed. By learning to allow her being to move and express itself freely she found a way of changing her habits of withdrawal. Because her suppression of her own pleasure left her feeling depressed, she had begun to believe she was ill in some way. The rapid change had dispelled those feelings and reaffirmed her self-confidence.

Maria approached coex with specific problems and they were dealt with even though she did not attempt to explore causes or analyse herself. Many people will find the same applies to them as well. This is because although they are not attempting an analytical approach, or 'concentrating' on the area of their difficulty coex itself often works at the causes of their problem automatically. In coex one is learning to use the process of self-regulation. This process is an automatic natural function dealing with imbalances anyway. So when we allow it to function more fully in coex, it may very well deal with the problem which concerns us. In any case, it is advisable to learn the general application of coex before attempting to guide it toward dealing with problem areas. This is not because one cannot guide it from the start, but simply that because it is something we learn, it is not worth trying to direct it until it is expressing itself fairly easily and fluidly. Once you find yourself at home with it, OR HAVE TRIED FOR SOME TIME AND CANNOT FIND FREE EXPRESSION, then try the specific methods described below.

Focusing on Specific Questions

The technique of FOCUSING, described by Eugene Gendlin in his book of the same name, I find a very helpful addition to the use of coex. Focusing seems to be an approach to the function of self regulation using certain steps. It is the steps which will be described here, as they are a great aid in looking at a specific problem or question in ones life.

Gendlin calls the stages MOVEMENTS. I will call them steps or stages so as not to create confusion when talking about coex movement reaction. The first stage is CLEARING A SPACE. To do this you start by asking yourself what is it that stops you from feeling satisfied with life, good and happy RIGHT NOW. You need to ask yourself this and be well and ready to respond fully and honestly. Do not hold back on any moans however small they may seem. State what they are and imagine putting them in a heap away from you, perhaps on the other side of the room. In stating your problem(s) in this way you may have just one thing you say, such as, "There's something wrong with the way I relate to work lately. I keep destroying the very things I'm trying to create." Or you might have a whole list of things such as, "My teeth ache a lot lately. Things would be okay if only I had a regular income. I begin to feel my age, and sometimes feel like I'm too tired to carry on. If my wife/husband wasn't constantly pressurising me life might improve too. Yes, and also, the damn roof has started leaking again."

Whatever there is to say, let it come out and stack it on the pile until you can say, "Yes, if it weren't for those I would feel okay." Until you reach that feeling keep emptying out your difficulties, and do not get hung up on any one of them by describing it at length. Stay reasonably detached, but do not hold back even a small grouse.

Gendlin describes the steps as if everyone has some sort of discomfort in their life. I wish to stress however that it may be that it is not a 'problem' you wish to explore, but a 'question'. And from my experience the question can be about anything which is important to you. So you could ask: Do I have any unexpressed preferences between choosing college or university? — There is something I am missing in what this patient is telling me – what is it? — I am working on the plot for my novel about the Star Wars crisis and it needs more drama – any ideas? My son is trying to decide a careers direction and has asked my help – what sense do I have from years of living with him? etc.

The second step is FINDING THE FELT SENSE OF THE PROBLEM OR QUESTION. From all that you have put out on the pile, is there one which feels worse or most pressing? Is there one which brings some sort of reaction like an ache in the belly, or a sense of stickyness or heavyness? If it is a question you have asked, see if there is a feeling or body movement which arises in connection with it. You can take that one to look at, or simply choose one you want to work on. Now use the same 'open screen' form of observation described in chapter two in exercise three. Notice what you are feeling in yourself, then take hold of the question/problem you have chosen and notice what changes occur on the screen of your body condition. Take the question/problem as a whole, not any one part of it. Consider what your feeling reaction is to it, not what you think about it. Have the open-being condition used to allow coex.

Gendlin's advice is particularly good at this point. He says that one may begin to experience a lot of 'static' from the mind as you enter this stage. You may begin to lecture yourself about the problem – "I simply haven't got what it takes at work. When will I admit it and give up trying to achieve something in life. It's like a disease I've got." Or you may begin to analyse the problem – "It all started back at school; no with my dad really, when I got into that authority struggle with him. Now I keep it up with anyone who I happen to feel is in charge." Or if it is a question – "I've never been able to figure this out, and talking to myself like a nut isn't going to help."

Drop the mental noise away, just as you have learnt to drop away the critical faculty to allow coex. Put it all aside for a while. This is a special thing you are doing, and you have hours in which to indulge in useless theorising later. Look inside to the feelings which exist beyond words. Maybe at first there is just emptyness. Never mind, watch it to see if a shift occurs. As you watch with the problem loosely held, your inner process will respond to it out of its mass of unconscious experience. Look at the place in yourself which has not yet been verbalised to see what feeling arises in response to the question you choose to look at.

A schoolteacher, Gerald, tried this technique just to see if it would work. He said he had no problems, was happily married, but was interested to find out if there was anything in the technique. When he got to the point of watching his inner screen he said he noticed a slight sensation in his chest. It was like a fluttery feeling, "nothing important." He would usually have passed it by as having no usefulness and no relevance to him. When I asked him to give it attention and allow it to develop, it moved to his throat. It then became a choking feeling and he cried. His tears were an expression of feelings he never normally allowed himself. In the school in which he worked, there was so much disinterest from the pupils in what was being offered by the teachers, that it moved him deeply to see how many of the children were wasting opportunies in their lives. His inner being was moved by the situation – however, he had not previously admitted this to himself. Of course you may feel there is no point in crying about something which, although it touches the very noblest feelings in you, cannot be altered. In denigrating this part of oneself however, it is well to remember such a life as that of Dr. Ignaz Semmelweis who discovered the cure for the fever (puerperal) which killed thousands of women at childbirth. Semmelweis did not dismiss the inner feelings he had when he watched women die in dozens in the hospital. His fellow doctors told him to ignore such foolish reactions. It was his feelings however, which drove him on to search for a cure.

Gerald's 'unimportant' fluttery feeling was the very way in which his non verbalised unconscious content was expressing itself. It is important not to denigrate such slight feeling changes or apparently unimportant movements. It is only by giving these previously ignored parts of oneself a chance to be known, that we form a link with the creative or healing response within us. Whatever the feeling situation is in this second stage, stay with it. Gendlin does not remark on the importance of allowing a movement response to the question, but this may exist even if no feeling is contacted. It may, as in Rhijn's explanation, be an expression of the question at a level outside of feelings. By allowing movement the feelings and insight may be able to form.

The third stip is FINDING A HANDLE. You need now to consider what is the quality of the feeling or movement. Can you put a word to it that fits? The word might be something like 'tight' - 'sleepy' – 'lost' – or anything descriptive which applies. Or it might be a short phrase such as, 'looking for something' – 'shutting people out' – 'almost grasping something'. If you have become quite expressive in coex, then it might be that you have spontaneous speech or words, or an image or scene comes to mind descriptive of what you are sensing inside. Andrew, who was exploring the reason for his lack of motivation in work, and had already discovered easy spontaneous vocalisation, experienced himself saying, "Pride was my only defence." He did not understand what the words meant, but let the question as to their meaning hang in his thoughts gently. He then quite quickly had a mental picture of his father showing him his school books. His father was saying, "Look how neatly I used to write. See – no blots. Look at these drawings, how much care I took over them. Why can't you keep your books clean and take care like that?" It was an actual memory of an event. Later Andrew contacted the feelings of humiliation he had felt as a youth in relationship with his father. He had used pride as a defence against feeling incapable and worthless. But he had stopped expressing himself in areas in which his father could criticise. This had continued into adult life. He had never put himself in a position where he could be criticised by an authority figure, which had curtailed his whole work creativity.

Do not force your word, phrase or image to fit your response. Just try different words until you find what feels right.

The fourth stage is RESONATING. Move backwards and forwards between your word or image and your inner feeling or movement. Do this until you sense you have made a satisfying connection. This is similar to exploring the image of the seed with body positions until you find one which fits. It is like the game one played as a child where something is hidden, then everyone shouts, 'Cold, colder, freezing!' as you move away, and 'Warm, warmer, boiling hot!' as you get closer.

When you do manage to 'resonate' a noticeable change occurs in what you are experiencing. Recently a person who was working told me afterwards, "I felt really lost and incapable of understanding why my life is as it is. Then when I found the word which described what was happening in me I felt a tremendous relief. It seemed almost as if being able to describe it clearly had cleared the problem." At this point one has not necessarily cleared the problem or found a clear response to the question, but it is certainly a step toward that. So when you can verbalise what you felt, give yourself time to respond to what arises, whether in changing feelings, movements or futher images.

The fifth stage is ASKING. When Andrew had got to the point of receiving the words, he was still not clear about what caused his work problem. He let the question as to what the words meant dangle in his thoughts without attempting to interfere with his spontaneous inner response. He did not let the 'static' and analysing process crowd in again. This is ASKING.

It may be that this stage of response comes very quickly as Andrew's did. Or it may take time to discover gradually the details of insight one seeks. Stay in the open receiving state however, without intellectualising, but certainly with curiosity and an asking frame of mind. The response may be in further movements, verbalisation, images or feelings. Perhaps many bits of information arise but you cannot get a cohesive, satisfying understanding. Recognise that you still do not understand, but remain open. If you persist, a point is reached where there is integration, you feel, often suddenly, that at last you understand. It is not that you have simply found a likely theory, you actually have a feeling of insight and satisfaction. In Gestalt this is called an 'Aha!' This is because one almost shouts out, Aha, I've got it!

Gendlin calls the sixth stage RECEIVING. This is more of an attitude than something that is done. It is a stance we take in relation to what has arisen, however little. The practice of coex is a form of active respect for the process of life in oneself and its innate wisdom and creativity. It is active because one has consciously to create a receptive attitude which honours the lifegiving inner forces. In successful use of coex we use the mental and physical functions which aid problem solving and our sense of social, enviromental and internal activities. When we ask a question of ourselves, and allow the process of coex to respond we are listening to what this sense tells us. This sense is not as immediate or as formed as our sense of sight, for instance. After all, what we are sensing is a complex web and interplay of forces both within ourself, as memories and biological activities, and around us as forces which are subtle – such as social pressure – but nevertheless very real. Although we sense these things, they are not at first formed into concrete visual images or intellectual concepts for our inspection. One has to listen for them, or reach out and touch as one would a gentle pulse. And this is important and fundamental in coex because, feeling that pulse, you will know you have a connection and a bond with the heart of things, both in yourself and beyond.

We need to honour whatever arises for us. Our unconscious does not lie to us. So whatever it presents needs to be honoured. When Andrew received the words about pride, he could not see how they related to him at all. But because he had learnt to trust his own process, he honoured them enough to continue 'receiving'. Even then, once he had remembered the event with his father, he still had not touched the feelings surrounding that event. That came in another session. So part of 'receiving' is to recognise that what arises may come in paragraphs. In our first session we may receive only an introduction to what we seek to understand or deal with . We do not need to believe or blindly accept what it is. Andrew did not believe or accept the words 'Pride was my only defence'. In a sense he said to himself, 'I don't know what this means, and I can't see how it applies to me. Nevertheless I accept there may be some relevance that I do not yet see, so I will continue with the question – What does this mean?' Do not negate or throw away what you have received in your session. As Gendlin says, do not let your negative criticisms "dump a truckload of cement on this new green shoot that just came up." The relationship with yourself takes time to develop and expand, just like any other relationship.

Hone the Inner Genius

After I had been using coex for a year and had a fluid response physically, emotionally, and vocally I tried using it as an aid in understanding particular questions important to me. I found that I received a response to whatever I sought to understand. Sometimes it was very little, sometimes full and helpful. Then one day, because I was working with physical education, I began a session in which I asked the question – Is there some form of exercise which would integrate the practitioner physically and emotionally? The response was so startling I found it difficult to believe. As if from a textbook, laid out in order and sequence, I began to receive the whole set of movements described in chapter three. So much detailed information came, which I spoke onto tape and still have, that I have only given the bare bones in this book. It took perhaps ten or more sessions to receive. Many of the concepts were quite new to me. They looked at the question I had asked from viewpoints I had never considered before. Some of the information was so new I could not remember it even a little while afterwards. As an experiment I asked for some of the details about energy movements in the pelvic area again without listening to the tape to refresh my memory. Out it flowed once more, and when I checked one against the other, there was no flaw. For the first time in my life I felt an awe for the possibilities available to us if we connect with the unconscious.

Over the years I found there are particular ways of working with this possibility that are helpful. Firstly your body, feelings and mind need to be capable of responding easily. Only in this way is it possible for what is held within yourself to express itself to consciousness. If you are not fluid in the use of coex, then the exercises given in chapter three need to be continued until you are.

Secondly, you need to put aside for a while what you consider to be possible or true. Consciously release yourself from the way you look at life, or the question in hand. If you have rigid views about politics, religion, society, or the subject you are trying to research, they act upon the formation of creative realisation just as a rigid tense body would act upon the expression of a dance. Relax them as much as possible.

Five years ago my wife, Hyone's, brother was living at Totnes, about a hundred miles from us. We decided to visit him and drove over the open moorland of Dartmoor. On our way back we stopped on the moor for a picnic and pee. Hyone realised she no longer had her glasses, but we could not remember whether she had had them since leaving her brother. Hyone thought she had and we searched the car, our picnic area, and the track and place she had gone to pee. I gave up after about fifteen minutes, but Hyone searched for much longer without success. When we arrived home we checked with her brother, but the glasses were not found. Nor did they turn up in the weeks that followed. It was seventy miles to where we had picnicked, so having searched so extensively already it did not seem worth returning for a casual search. But we were faced by the decision – was it worth while returning to search, or should Hyone buy new glasses. As they were specially tinted they would cost about £70. We decided to use coex to ask where the glasses might be. Hyone had never used coex in this way before. As she began her body started moving and bending. She almost stopped the action with the thoughts of, 'What possible use can this be?' She relaxed the thought and continued, and her body went into a squatting position.

Meanwhile I had similar negative reactions in the way of feelings suggesting this was a hopeless quest and a waste of time. I dropped the feelings though, and quickly had images of a low bank and the glasses under a bush on the bank. When we compared our experiences they tallied. Hyone's squatting she realised was suggesting the place where she squatted to pee. My bank was by the side of that very place. We drove there that day. Under the heather on the bank of the place she had squatted to pee, slightly covered in snow, lay her glasses.

If our already formed concepts that it was pointless to ask our unconscious where the glasses were had been allowed to dominate, we would not have been able to re-ceive the impressions we did. Also, we each received our impressions in a different way. Hyone's was purely in physical movement, while mine was in images. This is why I suggest bringing as much of ourself to the process of coex as we can. With body, voice, emotions, sexuality, and mind, there is more likelihood that some part of us can express what we need to know. Perhaps, as with Hyone, the reply comes in the form of mime. So we need to be open to look for the way the reply arises. In other words, if the body acts out something in movements, and you are looking for the response in the form of mental knowing, then you may think you have failed.

Supposing the response comes but you do not under-stand it; then you need to work with the coex response just as you would with someone with whom you were conversing. If you have not clarified what you are seeking to understand, ask for clarification and 'receive' the next response. If that too is not clear enough, ask again in a back and forth response. If you clarify some of what you are looking for but some remains out of reach, return to it in another session.

Do not forget that you are working with the forces of creativity. Sometimes the answer lies ready made within yourself, waiting to be let into consciousness. But sometimes what you seek is on the furthest edge of your knowing, or of your ability to live or understand. To receive it you must grow as a person, you may even have to carve the answer out of unformed experience. How many creative geniuses have left their masterpiece in the world without hard work, without facing and resolving conflicts of decision, without feeling deeply? Even when the work is first done, it may need revision after revision to shape it to what the artist wants. At our own level we are all creative geniuses. Our field of creativity may be helping to grow the unfolding personality of our children. It may be in meeting the ever changing demands of a commercial market. We might be a doctor attempting a fuller insight into a patient; or simply ourselves facing the challenge of existing and surviving. Therefore if the answer does not come ready made, take up the challenge of your life. If you do, you will create something with your life that would otherwise have been unsaid. In its present situation, humanity needs that type of creative genius.

Something I have seen which often frustrates the creative potential of coex is an attitude linked with being gullible. Let me take the example of someone I will call Sally. Sally has gained a good degree of mobility in allowing a spontaneous response. Whatever arises however, she neatly fits into her preconceived ideas. At no time does she say, 'I don't understand what that was about.' This is like me saying to Sally, 'The other day I met someone and I immediately disliked them. So Sally says, 'Oh, that must be because you knew each other in a past life.' That does not bring any insight to me, and although I want to explore the event to find an understanding which I can observe to fit what happened, Sally closes herself to any further communication. In this way Sally makes her sessions of coex say just whatever she wants them to say. They express exactly what she wants to believe. They do not rob her of the supports she emotionally craves. Due to her need to feel in control, she will believe that coex is healing any breakdown which occurs in her body. For Sally this works to the extent that she copes with the difficulties of her life because of the support of her beliefs. But as far as creativity is concerned it robs her of the opportunity to stand confounded by life. She may never know the wonder of unveiling from within herself a completely new view of things. With a mind already made up, she will never find what she did not already know. It also leaves her unclear of where her boundaries are in a real sense. If she believes her body is healing when it is not, she will not take the creative leap of looking for something that actually works. Such a leap means that we are ready to admit our present approach is inadequate, let go of it, and open to the new. Creativity constantly demands that of us. So if we are to use coex for such an end, we must be aware of our connection with what we already accept and believe, and hold it loosely.

Healing the Body

I began using coex partly because I was ill. I have learnt since then that I was ill because over a long period of time I had bottled up frustrations, hurts, love and tensions. As these were released or acknowledged the illness cleared. My present use of coex acts now like a preventative measure rather than a healing agent. It is like practising hygiene daily instead of trying to heal skin sores due to not washing. The tensions, the creative drives and feelings, instead of bottling up, are frequently met and dealt with. Because the prime aim of our self regulatory process is to maintain physical and psychological health, it is usually enough to use coex in a general sense, for its action to start improving our health. The homeostatic action will use all its resources if we are working with it.

John, a 54 year old television reporter, had experienced years of illness, including T.B.. Describing his experience of coex he says:

The body postures and movements were near miraculous to me because during the previous nine years, two serious accidents and a disease had resulted in five separate spinal fractures. For a period I had been encased from hips to jaw in a metal and leather support harness. For years I had endured great pain, and never in my prayers for help had I really hoped for the return to mobility of movement which is now shown in my childlike coex play movements.

The return of mobility is only one of the blessings I have enjoyed since beginning coex. For many years I had experienced consistently poor health; a lifetime of asthma compounded by T.B. in both lungs, and poor digestion with its attendant consequences, had all produced a dismal attenuation of minimal well-being with serious illness. In the first four weeks of coex I felt great draughts of air pouring into my lungs. At the end of eighteen months my chest had expanded by four inches, which I discovered when I bought new underwear. My spine moved more freely than it had for years. My indigestion, with its accompanying constipation, disappeared. I am fitter than I have been for the previous forty five years.

Ann, a married woman with three children, approached coex from a different health situation than John. She explains her situation as follows:– "After practising coex for nearly two and a half years there are considerable physical changes of which I am aware. They are not dramatic in the sense of 'pick up thy bed and walk', but have come about gradually.

I was always a very cold person – I felt shrivelled up with cold, and wore numerous jerseys to keep warm. I ached with cold, and being thin I felt this keenly. However, I haven't worn a vest now for a year, I am far more often warm than cold, and feel so much more alive because of this. My feet were usually cold – now even though I wear sandals they are warm. I feel so much more energy and joy of living. I feel it flow through me.

I used to have a permanently sore and red throat. I was often sick with diarrhoea for 48 hours at a stretch, several times each year. I feel these were due to tension. I was verbally suppressed as a child. Now if my throat feels sore I realise I am withholding my speech. The diarrhoea I think was a way of releasing tension which I no longer need. In coex I was able to release my feelings in words, and I was often led to chanting and singing. Although I am not completely released in this area yet, my voice is already lower and more relaxed.

Other things are that I used to tilt my head on one side a great deal, and kept my shoulders permanently raised. This was accompanied by shallow breathing and hand clenching. These have gone now, and my digestion, which was 'delicate' has altered too. I can digest raw vegetables and fruit skins easily, and because of this I eat and enjoy more useful foods. Yet again it happened slowly and almost unnoticeably over two years. Perhaps that is not slowly though, when I had been suffering for nearly 30 years.

Before I started coex I considered myself to be a 'normally functioning person', not a freak. I don't know how I went on year after year imposing such strain on my system – but I did. It was not until I had used coex for two and a half years that I began to understand what real living is. Not manipulated by fears and tension. Not 'putting on' a self in the morning. Sometimes now I find myself off centre. But I know now when this is happening so can watch to see why. I live more fully from what I call my intuitive centre, and begin to instinctively know what I need, and follow it. Best of all though is having MYSELF, which is so wonderful!

John and Ann practised their coex in slightly different ways. John started by practising with the guidance of someone teaching him. He then began to practise alone at home. Ann first began coex in a group in Exeter. She then felt she needed individual help, so worked with a teacher.

Health is not simply being able to jog for a couple of miles, or bend and touch ones toes. Our being cannot be split into neat compartments of body health and mental health. Every thought acts directly within the body, often leading it into dynamic action. When coex is working in us, it uses therapeutic tools I have never heard applied in straight psychotherapy. It does not have the limitations of a theoretical school to bind it, so its action uses whatever is appropriate. This may be movements of a regular sort, posture, strange jerks, or dancing. But it may deal with our health by mobilising our feelings and mental health. Here is a description by Mark of a session of this type.

> Started this session very quickly, singing in what sounded like a foreign language, and foot stamping. The song wasn't coming out very well, and my right arm began to swing round and round. This seemed to lead me into bark-like sounds and from there into full African singing. I don't think I have ever sung as noisily or as lustily as I did in this session. Gradually the singing chant became more and more forceful and fluent. I surrendered into it deeply and a torrent of words poured out. I really felt like an African Chief chanting to a great crowd of people – not just because of the sounds, but because my feelings were flowing. The chant became even more forceful, filling the hall with sound, and finally in a tremendous roar or bellow, I called out, just as if warriors had been roused, and the roar sent them on their way to battle.

This type of chanting is fairly common in coex. It is a well known phenomenon connected with the unconscious, often known as 'glossolalia', sometimes called speaking in tongues, and recorded for thousands of years. My experience of it suggests it is the way the unconscious expresses its feeling contents prior to understandable verbalisation. So in Van Rhijn's scale it would be an expression of level three. The streaming feelings which usually accompany this spontaneous chanting act to cleanse and balance ones inner life. I can only talk from my impression of this, but it seems to act similarly to circulation. If we sit a lot our circulation becomes sluggish. A brisk walk will stimulate circulation and help clear away waste products and activate cell growth in muscles and bones. Similarly, if our feelings are not stimulated frequently, they need this flowing activity to clear away negative feeling debris, and promote a healthy soul. In this way the many facets of our energy and feelings move into a fuller, freer expression of themselves. They feel like exercises of the soul.

Jung says that our psyche is both male and female. The man, he shows, also has a female side to his psyche, and the woman a male side. From the above experiences it seems likely that although we may be born a white male or a black female, we also have within us the characteristics not only of the opposite sex, but also of other racial types, as well as animals, plants and minerals. Jung says that a lot of illness occurs when the secondary sexual characteristics are suppressed, and we become unbalanced. Balance seems to be when the different aspects of our being, including the minerals in our bones, the vegetative processes in our cells, the animal behaviour patterns in our unconscious, the opposite sexual characteristics, are balanced and in a reasonable degree integrated into our waking personality.

Ann's experience is an example of how a great deal of ill health and poor functioning is caused by living with a lot of unconscious tension. Ann was a very courageous and hard worker as far as coex is concerned, and was willing to face many experiences she had previously bottled up inside herself. To give some sort of understanding of what this means I will quote Ann at length regarding one aspect of her coex. She says that "During one coex session I was deeply involved in re-experiencing parts of several of my children's births. These experiences all centred on surgical shocks, to which at the time I accepted passively, but which when I re-experienced them, were more fully understood by me to have been terrifying assaults on my body and threats to my yet unborn babies.

The first one was a surgical induction of my third baby and I deeply felt that as the doctor thrust a pair of scissors inside my vagina that he would pierce my baby. In coex I could feel the terror which engulfed me but which I had not allowed myself, or had not been allowed by the hospital setting, to feel and react to. This time I was able to shout and cry out – 'Don't; don't do it, you'll hurt my baby!' and I let out the fullness of my feelings.

But the strangest experience was of my son's birth. I had never fully understood what it meant. It was a blurred and painful memory for me, until this session, when so much was made clear. It was a Caesarian birth, followed by my sterilisation in hospital. It sounds straightforward, and technically it probably was. But a part of my being was numbed by the strangeness, the unreality of this birth. I could not feel that my son was born because I had not experienced the birth pains. I was like a bewildered animal at times, asking for him. 'Have I had my bady?' I asked the nurses. They looked at me very oddly – they didn't understand. At night I got up and looked for him. I had to hold him, in order to believe.

After his birth he was kept from me for two days for a thorough examination. I was frantic with longing to hold him – I even made my way along the endless length of corridor to search for him – although I was hardly able to walk. In the end I was taken in a wheelchair to see him through a glass window. My whole being ached for him. In the session I screamed for him and sobbed, 'he's mine, he's mine' over and over again. When I did have him I wasn't allowed to feed him because I had recently had T.B. It was such a deep blow to my motherhood. At the time I was mute with anguish – now I released the words I had longed to say. I felt that my son had been taken away from me. Taken from my womb, taken to the examination room; taken from my breast; taken even by my husband. The nurse fed him with a bottle, flicking the soles of his feet to make him suck. I saw my husband pick him up. 'At last I have a little son' he said. His joy was a delight I couldn't share. He was my fourth baby and all the other births had been occasions of great joy. I didn't understand the clinical Caesarian birth, and all the surrounding complications which enveloped me. I felt such coldness, such a lack of understanding. It was against my nature. Against my instinctive mother longings. No one explained that this unnatural birth might bring such feelings.

In looking at and re-experiencing these birth traumas, I am more and more sure that during childbirth women have an extra sensory awareness, an aura of sensitivity which surrounds them and makes them alert to any threat to their baby. So when any surgical assault is made on their bodies at this time, any artificial or interfering gesture, even an injection – it is very deeply felt. I don't think that enough is understood of the primitive, instinctive side of childbirth.

Six days after my son's birth I passed out. When I awoke on my bed I was sobbing from the core of my being. I was engulfed in my crying for a long period of time – tears broke from me in waves. Then I thrashed about and screamed. At one point I was above my bed looking down on myself lying there. I let go completely. But of course I was injected with tranquilising drugs, calmed down and held down. After that I was given tranquilisers three times a day and I became a good, quiet, well-behaved patient. But there was so much seething inside me, kept down – I now understand – so that only in this coex session seven years later could I see that my sterilisation had killed my creative energy – could I feel my maternal creative energy had been destroyed, tied up inside me, killed – could I understand how I resented the death of my precious pregnancies. I had flowered so sweetly during my pregnancies. Now they were gone. I even resented my husband for it, because he had agreed it as a good idea. I could no longer enjoy intercourse for the sadness hung over me – but I hadn't understood this at the time. Outwardly I accepted it – inwardly I pined.

I went to a psychiatrist for treatment for deep depression after I returned home. I felt so guilty too as I could read the reproaches in people's eyes – 'she has a beautiful little son, and she's depressed.' I was given more drugs, first stimulants then tranquilisers – and told that it would pass, that time is a great healer. I learnt to live on my tranquilisers for the first five years, until I began coex and gave them up. Then after two years of coex I uncovered the truth – and I feel that although I can never give my son those things that were missing at the time, I can now really accept my sorrow and can build from there. I also feel that my creative energies are beginning to flow again in other channels.

In moving toward health using coex, unless your condition is a simple one which needs self help rather than professional direction, it is wise to work with the guidance of your doctor. At least check out whether your condition is directly physical or psychosomatic. If it is physical, like an infection, coex can help, but one obviously needs to follow common sense as well, such as sufficient rest and a healthy diet. Coex is an expression of your own innate healing function. If it worked perfectly no one would be ill anyway. Cooperating with it increases its efficiency, but it only occasionally achieves miracles. Anyway, miracles are only the functioning of a natural law which we have perhaps not yet defined.

If your illness does not respond to coex, you need to suspect that there are suppressed past experiences which have not yet been released. Ask what it is, and be ready to work via symbols to start with. Ann took two years to unearth some of her most important tensions. It is seldom the hardest we release first. However, some ill health or difficult feelings – perhaps the largest percentage – are due to habits. Habits to do with eating, with exercise, with the way we react to situations, and the way we tangle up or smooth our inner energies. Because coex gradually expands our awareness of ourselves, these habits become notice-able. Of course, that does not magically banish them. Only your own skill and persistence in re-creating yourself can do that.

Creative Imagination Coex and Health

Ann's discovery that a particular time of her life was the 'site' of her tension is applicable to most of us. Sometimes the cause of the tense state occurred in a period of time lasting only a few minutes. I remember a conversation with my mother about masturbation which lasted a minute at the most. Although it was short it so terrified me – with great emotion she told me masturbation would certainly kill me – that the results of it lasted thirty years. Some-times what troubles our inner functioning has entered us over a longer period such as puberty, or the years of marri-age to one partner. Or it may be the sum total of a relation-ship with one person such as our father.

If we seek to release these areas of tension, one way we can approach coex is to work through our life consecu-tively. I am not suggesting that in one clean sweep we can remove the tensions in our lives. Left to itself the uncon-scious tends to deal with whatever is 'loose' first, or nearest the surface. It jumps from one age or life period to another, backwards and forwards, clearing a bit here, rebuilding there. So when we attempt to organise it consecutively it will not completely comply as it has its own rhythms. The point of working in this way however, is to purposefully recognise that certain areas of our life may need renovating, and starting the process of bringing awareness to them.

Therefore, what I suggest, once you are mobile in coex, is to list the moments or periods of your life when there were obvious or possible difficulties. On the list should be put any times in hospital, especially as a child away from its mother; birth of a younger brother or sister; puberty; death of parent or someone very close; major accidents; difficult times of relationship with a parent or home; birth; times when you heard something negative about yourself, such as your mother saying she tried to abort you. List these out in sequence and, starting from the one nearest in time work back through them.

The way to do this is that where possible, such as with birth and operations, take the physcial position connected with the situation. It does not matter if this is simply your imaginative concept of what the position should be. Hold the thought of the event and let free movement and fantasy arise. Do not concern yourself with whether what arises actually took place. It may do, it may not. To test whether people do have memories of early childhood Dr. Cheek used hypnosis. While deeply relaxed his subjects were asked to remember what position their head was in at birth. Their response was checked against their medical records and found to be 100% correct. Nevertheless, it is not a wise thing to get stuck in expecting 'correct' memories. The unconscious often needs to release its 'fantasies' about some area of our life. Even though these are not actual memories, they are just as healing, sometimes more so. After all, it may not have been the event that disturbed us. It may have been our feeling reaction to it, or our imagination about it, which created misery and tension in us.

To work wisely in this way we must not forget that only a small portion of our being is a conscious, rational, entity. We are largely a biological and feeling creature which may be tied up by many invisible but potent influences. I remembcr working with a young girl who had a terror of injections. When she was relaxed I suggested she remember the cause of her fear and experience the feelings of it. She allowed her spontaneous response to this, and re-enacted a scene in which she was visiting a hospital out-patients department to receive an injection for an allergy she suffered. It was to be an intravenous injection, but the nurse could not hit the vein, so was injecting again and again...and again. The girl was calling for her mother who stood some feet away. The mother did not respond because she was held by the invisible bonds of respecting the authority of the nurse and wanting her daughter to have the injection. The girl wanted to fight and run away but was held by wanting to comply with her mother's judgement, and not wanting to fight with the nurse. Out-side those bonds, she, as a nutural creature would have screamed, fought, and attempted to run away. Holding back the urges to do so created tension and fear in her. Her organism, or her being, needed to allow the urges to be expressed. Therefore, when you approach any event in your life through coex, drop what you think ought to happen, and simply let your organism express what it needs to. Perhaps it will not stick to social niceties, but that is a part of healing. There is no fear of the unsocial expres-sion spreading beyond the session. But if you cannot allow your being to relax from all the social do's and don'ts sometime, you are bound to build up tension.

During each session, allow yourself to express whatever arises. If you do not feel you have completed whatever was happening, come back to what you were considering at other sessions until you arrive at a peacefulness. Some-times this takes a number of sessions, sometimes just one. Once completed however, move on to the next event to be worked on. As already said, the reason for working in this way is to begin the process of extending awareness into parts of our experience where tension and hurt may be. Therefore, once you have worked back through your list, you can either practice coex without direction; or you may have become aware that certain areas need more work.

Because doctors, nurses and therapists do not have unlimited time in which to work with each individual patient, the use of coex has a very real part to play within the healing techniques used today. By teaching the fundamentals of it to patients; by helping them to accept the need their organism has to express itself in this way, and by creating an environment in which an individual or group can use coex, a great deal can be done to reduce stress and stimulate positive health in patients.

CHAPTER 5

The Dream and Coex

In general, and even from medical and psychological viewpoints, there is a blind spot in regard to the dream process and the action I have outlined under the name of coex. Because of the blind spot there is very little 'trust' in the ability of our organism to heal itself, to solve its own problems, or to act creatively outside the conscious rational mind. During the time my wife and I worked for The Daily Mail as dream interpreters, we collected thousands of dreams. One of the things which struck us as we studied the dreams was how few of them arrived at solutions to difficulties arising in the dream. Considering the almost awesome problem solving faculties of the unconscious this suggests we are culturally untrained in, or out of touch with, our own potential in this area.

Working as a psychotherapist for many years, using coex as the basis for my work, I observed how many therapists leave no room for the clients internal process and creativity to be expressed. It was during these years I realised first about the blind spot people have to their own possibilities. This is very clearly stated by S.M. Chrem in his thesis, *The Role of Energy In The Psychotherapeutic Process*. He says:

> It seems to us that although the body therapies described above, claim to practise organismic self-regulating techniques, all of them have highly developed structures in their therapeutic approaches. The least structured approaches in which the process of self-regulation is much more respected are best exemplified by the work of David Boadella and Tony Crisp. Although they have a wide range of techniques to apply when necessary the client plays the most active role. These therapists trust in

the self-regulative process and follow the client, waiting for the development of his process. This attitude serves as a model for the client, who soon starts to trust in his own internal spontaneity and the creativity of his un-conscious. With the arousal and amplification of the involuntary movements, gestures symbols or words, spontaneous activity is integrated with consciousness, will and analytic power. The therapist who applies the self regulative approach establishes contact with the client and accepts him as he is.

Lastly, I would like to briefly mention an intense ex-perience which I lived through within the therapeautic context of my training course in Bioenergetics led by David Boadella and Helen Davis. In this experience I could feel how physical, emotional and mental aspects reflect and influence each other, functioning as a whole.

It was in a workshop run by Tony Crisp. I was work-ing on a dream I had had many times in the previous two years. During this work, not only did I experience the energy flowing in my body, from my head down to the tip of my toes, as a pleasurable and relaxed sensa-tion, but I also felt a sensation of freedom during the process. My movements were easy and coordinated. I experienced these movements as a dance. I felt that the energy flowing through my body directed my move-ments. I began to express different sounds and to laugh noisily. I was truly happy. I had awareness of my inner potential. I had a clear, complete and vivid image of my body and there came to my mind flashes of scenes that I had lived in different moments of my life.

I felt that the good rapport that I had with the ther-apist was very important for me to express some parts of my being which had been buried for a long time. I felt deep gratitude to Tony who accompanied me and allowed me to go through this process of self discovery.

For me this experience was very significant from the therapeutic point of veiw. It gave me a great confidence in the self-regulative process for my body and simul-taneously provoked a change in my mental attitude. That is, I was more open to feeling and sensations as well as flexible and adaptable to different situations.

Moving into the Dream

If a dream is an expression of the same process we meet in coex, then it is clear that if we approach a dream we are already confronting deep and spontaneous activities of our inner being. In 1985 I helped a woman, Marilyn, to use coex in regard to the pain and anxiety she was experiencing about her impending divorce. Marilyn had dreamt of seeing a dinosaur standing in her path, devouring all who approached it. The dream was a part of her own self-regulatory process which was easily available to work with. So we explored it by having Marilyn find a body posture and movements which for her expressed the feeling of the dinosaur. By doing this we gave more attention or consciousness to what might otherwise have remained an apparently unimportant part of her experience – the dream.

In her experiment with posture and feelings, Marilyn did not sense anger or aggression, but she did feel like a predator which always had to TAKE to gain her own needs. This feeling immediately reminded her of her family life as a child. She remembered one time when she was sent shopping as a very young child of three or four, and as well as buying what she had been asked, she purchased some sweets for herself. When she arrived home she was treated as if she had done a terrible thing, and that was when she began to feel like a predator. It seemed to her as if her own needs were always gained at the expense of someone else.

With this awareness, she could now see that the dinosaur standing in her path clearly related to her present situation. Bargaining to gain a realistic share of the house and property jointly owned by her husband and herself, felt to her as if she were gaining her needs at his expense, like a predator. That made her feel so awful, she was almost ready to allow her husband to take all, leaving her without a house or money to start again. Her awareness of where the feelings arose from however, and the unrealistic part they played in her life, allowed her to relate to the situation with less pain and more wisdom.

There were two main ways Marilyn gained insight from

her dream. Firstly she took on the physical posture of the dinosaur – inasmuch as she could. From that starting point she allowed herself to spontaneously express body movements, etc. So she was giving the coex process a key starting point by holding the posture and thinking of the dream. Also, when she allowed spontaneous movement her unconscious was enabled to 'comment' on the dream, add to it, or continue it – and by continue I here mean bring it nearer to conscious understanding. One might, for instance, in intellectually considering the meaning of the dinosaur, think of it as an angry beast. When Marilyn explored her feelings and spontaneous expression of the creature, she found it not to be angry but all – devouring. the subtle difference between the two was important for her in enabling her to define what it portrayed of herself.

When Marilyn reached points where she could gain no further insight another approach was used. I asked her to imagine that she stepped into the body of the dinosaur and see what it 'felt' like. If this was unclear I suggested she swung between being herself and being the dinosaur, and compare the difference between the two states. In our dreams we often create people or objects which are important. The approach of standing in the very form of the person or thing, using the 'open screen' technique described in chapter two, and noting changes of feeling, is a way of grasping very subtle and basic qualities being expressed in the dream. By themselves the movements and feelings may not bring insight into the dream. What happened for Marilyn was that once she had become aware of the 'predator' feeling it immediately recalled to mind her experience as a child. So in working in this way one must leave the doors of ones being open, so to speak, to allow these associated memories and realisations to emerge. Therefore it helps if the question is in the back of ones mind as to what connection the movements, words or arising feeling, have with past or present experience. Do not be content with a purely intellectual understanding or interpretation. When you find real insight into a dream it will be accompanied by something of a thrill or feeling of satisfaction, and there will be little or no room for doubt that the dream has been unveiled.

Do You Like Eating People?

While Hyone and I were working at the holistic summer community of Atsitsa on the Greek island of Skyros, we learnt another approach to dreams which has proved to be extremely useful. Dina Glouberman, director of the community, and Senior Lecturer in Social Psychology at Kingston Polytechnic, taught us her 'creative visualisation' approach to the self regulatory process of the unconscious. It is extremely straightforward and effective. When we applied it to dreams it added an extra helpfulness to gaining insight. It can be used while one is exploring the dream symbol as Marilyn was doing through body movement and posture, or simply through speech. In fact the method is to work with a partner or group who ask you questions based on the symbol on which you are working.

If Marilyn were working in this way, we might ask her such questions as:– Do you like eating people?...What does it feel like being a dinosaur?...Are you eating everything because you are hungry?...Are you a young dinosaur? The questions should not take Marilyn away from what she is exploring, but lead her into identification with her symbol. They need to be simple questions. The strength of Dina's approach is in its ability to lead one into watching how we respond to our dream image through the stimulus of the questions. For instance, when we first used the technique with a dream group I was leading at Atsitsa, I was exploring my own dream image of a house. The members of the group asked me such questions as: Are your doors open to let people in?...Are you light or dark inside?...Are you a new or old house?...Are you a house to live in or a business premises? I found that with most of the questions I had a clear feeling response to them. As the house I was quite sure, out of how I felt, as to whether I liked people in me or not, how old I was, and what my function was. Out of the replies I gave, a clearer insight into how I personally felt about people, about whether I was 'open' to people 'entering' my life, etc, was defined for me.

In teaching her technique Dina explained that it is easier for people to talk about the house/dog/dinosaur and their depth of feelings and reactions to life, than it is to respond to the same questions about themselves personally. Therefore, it is most helpful only to come back to what the questions reveal to us about ourselves after we have fairly fully explored the symbol. Also, if any particular question arouses feelings or more than usual response, it is helpful to stay around the topic of the question for some time. For instance, if a question about age evokes a strong response, then other question such as – Is it difficult being the age you are?...Do dinosaurs of your age have special problems to face? – need to be asked.

If the questions are being asked while the person is exploring spontaneous movement, they need to be slanted to what is happening as well. So one could ask – Show me how dinosaurs eat things...What is that movement expressing? etc.

Whatever way you choose to work with dreams using the action of coex, it is important to remember the differences between dream action while asleep, and possible change while awake. Freud pointed out that we take feelings of guilt or fear into our dreams, and there repress what might otherwise be openly and explicitly expressed. His examples were the use of keys, locks, fingers, to represent sexual activity. In such cases sex was symbolised because of fear or guilt instead of being directly experienced in the dream. What we allow into our conscious personality is a highly edited version of what we feel and have impulse to do within ourselves. While the unexpurgated version of ourselves is certainly more varied than our conscious edited edition, it is certainly not a monster, as suggested by Dr. Jekyll and Mr. Hyde. It is, in fact, a more balanced and rounded self. What we repress is not only our sexuality or our pain. As is suggested by the experience of Dr. Semmelweis already quoted, we might also repress our noble instincts of caring and empathy.

Each of us has habits regarding what we edit out of our behaviour and conscious life. Some people edit any urge toward violence for instance, while for some people violence is their profession. Whatever our habit, we carry it into our dream life. It might be that our habit is to edit any emotion. In such a case, even if our spouse dies, we may not allow ourselves to cry our grief while awake. Because the habit is carried into our dreams, we find it hard to release our feelings even there. So the attempt on the part of the dream process to bring psychological balance through self-regulatory release is stifled. Recent studies of the connection between repressed emotion and the incidence of cancer, suggest the seriousness of this type of editing.

The reason these points are mentioned is because uniting dream-work with coex enables us to over-ride some of our editing habits. While asleep it is difficult to notice where our habits are causing negative side effects or killing our creativity. While awake and allowing the conscious dreaming of coex, we still have our critical faculties alert enough to see where negative editing is taking place and re-evaluate the process. In my INSTANT DREAM BOOK, I mention how Roger faced his habit of feeling anxious about what 'might' happen in his life. Because of his anxiety Roger avoided taking risks in regard to his work. Although he felt frustrated he stayed in a safe job because of this. In recognising his habit however, he began to be able to allow creative drives in himself which would require him to take risks. Although it promised no regular wage, he started free lance work in which he could express some of his own ideas.

Marilyn's dream work also illustrates how she was able to recognise her habitual response and change it into something more satisfying. Her habitual response was to feel like a predator when it came to asking for what she needed. Her re-evaluation of this was to see herself as having been led to the predatory feelings by others in her childhood, and to recognise her present needs as valid. This enabled her to seek them with more confidence.

If it is repressed emotions or insight we are dealing with, because it is our habit to repress them we will confront this habit as we work on a dream which contains them in symbols. In other words, because we repress the emotion we neither express it in waking or dream it openly, but symbolise it instead. While working on the dream we may come to the point of realising the symbol represents our feeling of grief, but we still do not feel the grief. Sometimes this critical point of change is typified by feeling as if one can go no further, or that 'nothing is happening'. Although one may have been working well on the dream before, the reason 'nothing happens' is because the habit of repression has come into play, blocking further fantasy or feeling. To overcome our habit and pass beyond this point we need to consciously decide to allow our feelings. This following dream and description of Margery L's, shows how feelings may be locked in us. She says:–

> My husband died suddenly four months ago. We had been married for 31 years. Ever since his death I've been trying to remember his face but cannot, which I find very queer and upsetting. I look at his picture but can't see him in my mind. However, last night, for the first time since his death I slept fairly well, and I dreamt of him. We were together in our back garden. Suddenly I spotted lots and lots of horrible slugs and started to kill them by treading them into the ground – there were also a lot crawling up the shed wall! 'Don't kill them', said my husband, 'everything has a right to life. They will probably do some good, and we mustn't kill them.' He looked at me so kindly and seemed so peaceful and happy. Then I woke up. Normally, in real life if he'd seen a slug in his garden he would have said, 'Fetch the salt Marge, that'll shift him!'
>
> What did this dream mean? I was brave all the days and months following his death. But lately I have been crying a lot, because it has suddenly struck me that I'll never see him again. But today I feel more at peace. Can you explain it?

The slugs are Margery's difficult feelings about her husband, which she has been vigorously killing. When she says she was 'brave', what she really means is that she was suppressing her feelings, which in the long run could have caused illness. The dream shows both her attitude of 'killing' the feelings, and also the change which allows her to cry and feel the resulting peace.

All the examples given of dreams show how a change can come about the way we view or deal with life through dream-work. The three factors responsible for this appear to be:–

1 Awareness of some aspect of ourselves is achieved. Through becoming aware of what reaction she had to gaining her needs, Marilyn could begin to avoid its negative consequences.

2 Releasing what was suppressed. Margery could begin to sleep again and feel at peace because the self-regulatory action in her dream helped her to allow the suppressed emotions for her husband.

3 Integration of our personality with the life processes which form it. By opening his personality to the forces active in his dream, Chrem found a change which resulted in greater trust in his own inner process and a sense of greater well-being. The forces in the dream were accepted and integrated into his personality.

CHAPTER 6

Teaching Coex

Coex can be as easily taught as relaxation, yoga or aerobics are at present. The concept of mental and physical health being achieved through an inner process being allowed expression is certainly not a widespread one in our culture. But for those who are ready to work with coex, I want to describe how they can teach it.

To teach coex well, one needs to have some background in practical psychological phenomena such as projection, resistances, and symbol formation. Useful books in this area are: *The Barefoot Psychoanalyst* by John Southgate and Rosemary Randall; *Getting Clear* by Anne Kent Rush; *Myself and I* by Constance Newland; *Modern Man in Search of a Soul* by Carl Jung; and LSD *Psychotherapy* by W.V. Caldwell. Just these few books are mentioned because if they are all read, a clear and broad view of human inner life is met. They deal not only with the wide variety of forces and factors which one might confront, but also give very clear and direct ways to deal with them.

I have known people who taught coex extremely well, who themselves never experienced its spontaneous release. Nevertheless, a deeper insight is acheived if one has used the process over a period of a year or more. There are, however, several ways you can present coex to others. My own first learning experience was in a peer group in which each person took responsibility for themselves. There was no 'teacher' in the sense of someone with experience who was showing the rest how to use the process. This approach is extremely useful with people who understand something of coex, and who wish to support each other in their use of it.

If you are already a teacher of a class which includes relaxation, dance, free movement, bio-energetics, or keep-fit exercises, coex can be usefully introduced into the pro-gramme. If the presentation is done carefully, the practi-tioners can find a helpful release of tension and self expres-sion, without entering into a depth of self exploration they do not seek. Even if you are organising a group specifically for the use of coex, the following guidelines are still useful.

Teaching Body Skills

1 For a useful and yet light-hearted approach to coex in a class situation, first explain that although most of our movements are deliberately made, our body also has a need to express itself spontaneously, as when we yawn and sneeze. Then introduce the technique of finding spontane-ous arm movements, as described in chapter two. This is where a hand is pressed against a wall.

Have the group use this several times and have fun with it, feeling their arm or arms float upwards. To help the group make more contact with each other and drop some of their inhibition about being together, have them try the experiment with a partner. The person who is trying the experiment stands with their arms by their side. The partner then holds their arms close to their side while they try to raise both arms. In this way they can try the experi-ment with both arms. After about thirty seconds, the experimenter relaxes, and the partner releases their hold.

If the group is new to coex, it is best to introduce one thing at a time, separated by the gap in time between the class meeting. It can be said to the class that what is being taught is a way of learning relaxation which is more helpful than the general 'lying on floor quietly' type. So after the group members have enjoyed having their arms rise, have them be aware of how their body 'feels' when they let their arms rise. In other words, there is a different feeling in their body from resisting the movement than allowing it. Have them explore the difference by resisting, then allowing, the movement. Then use what they have learnt by asking them to created the feeling of 'allowing' in their whole body, and slowly, without losing the feeling, find a position of rest in which they can let themselves drop into that feeling more fully.

2 What is being presented is an integrated approach to relaxation and stress release. Also the class are gently learning to listen to their feeling sense and follow it to their own benefit. Therefore, the next step to build in their awareness of coex is to have the group work as pairs to deepen the experience of allowing or letting go. This will be called 'allowing' or the 'open state' for ease of explanation.

Because many tensions are habitual and unconscious, it is a great aid to work with a partner to learn the type of relaxation mentioned above. It helps us drop tensions we might otherwise miss. To start, ask the class to choose a partner and have one person lie down with their partner kneeling by their side. Have the person who is the subject take time to settle, and bring awareness in turn to the legs, trunk, arms, neck and head to let go of unnecessary tension. Ask them to tell their partner when they feel relaxed.

The partner should then help deepen the awareness of the relaxed state by taking one of the subject's hands and, lifting it. This should be done with attention as to whether: [a] The arm is completely free and limp. [b] The arm is reasonably relaxed but at times the person either unconsciously tries to help in making the movement, or tenses against what you are doing. [c] The arm is very tense and resists movement.

The aim of the helper is to increase the awareness of the subject, and sometimes act as a mirror for what is happening. As already stated, many tensions are unconscious. This means that they are occuring spontaneously outside the direction of the conscious mind. So, when the helper takes the subject's hand, and moves their arm, the subject's attempt to help, or their tension against the movement may happen whether they will it or not. The subject will probably not be able to let go of these tensions even if they attempt to – that is, not at first. Because these tensions are unconscious habits, happening outside conscious direction, the first aim is to help in bringing them to the awareness of the subject.

As the group leader it is helpful to demonstrate the technique first. So if the subject is able to relax their arm easily, you need to say something like, "Are you aware of how fully you are relaxing your arm? Can you allow that feeling of letting-go to pervade the rest of your body?" If the subject attempts to help the movement, or blocks at certain points, then say, "As I move your arm are you aware of the attempt to help me make the movement?" Or, "Can you feel the tension at this point as I move your arm?" The same applies if the arm is very tense. The subject may be quite sure they are very relaxed until you move their arm. Even then they may not immediately know the degree of their tension. Therefore, you must help them gain awareness of it – really feel the tension.

It helps to move the arm through it's whole range of movement, pointing out areas of tension, and focusing on the area until the subject becomes aware of where the tension exists. Once you have worked with each arm separately, move both arms together in random activity, giving the subject time to gradually experience some of their tensions during the movement. Or if there is no resistance, let them deepen their ability to relax during movement. Give people a chance to talk about what they have experienced and how they view it. When you bring the subject's attention to points of resistance, the resistance or rigid tension will not immediately go. Tensions are rooted a lot deeper than our conscious will, often growing out of previous experience and unconscious reactions to past events. They are habits, and as such need to be gradually transformed. The first step is to become aware of the tension(s). Secondly, through subject and helper working together, the subject can practice the feeling of letting-go. The growth in this is measurable in how much one resists movement made by the helper. Therefore, through this simple technique we can teach members of a group how to have an immediate insight into how well they have learnt to relax. Through practice the ability to 'allow' is increased. Learning this is a body skill. The practitioners feel in their bodies, they learn in their muscles, how to drop tension. It is not simply a mental event. Therefore, if you are the teacher, in giving information to the subject, you are partly aiming at leading them to feel/learn in their body, what it is like to let go of resistances while being moved. Sometimes a tension is holding back a lot of energy/emotion. As the tension is melted, the energy will be released in the form of muscular twitches, movements, shivering, feelings, or imagery.

It helps the class to learn the new body feeling of allowing if contrasts are given. Therefore, after moving the arms in the way described, have the subject now actively resist while the helper moves both arms. The resistance should not be so strong as to become a great struggle, just enough to allow the person to compare the feeling of letting-go, to that of active resistance. Get the subject to swing between resisting and letting-go. This helps to define as a body skill the ability to let go of resistance. Ask the subject and helper to work together having the subject swing between the feeling of allowing and active resistance. The subject should particularly note the different feel of this in their body. Practising these types of 'body feeling' helps the subject to be much more aware of them. They are brought more fully into conscious direction, and are a powerful beginning to developing the sense of ease in using coex.

Although it has taken some time to describe this, the use of it in class, once it has been learnt, need only take about ten minutes. Then the helper should change roles with the subject. The aim is still to increase awareness of the feeling sense and the experience of 'allowing'. Just as this was carried into use in finding a relaxed position of rest, so the same should be done at the end of this teaching session also.

3 The next stage in teaching this is to bring what has been learnt into everyday activities, and is best given after the previous stage has been practised for a couple of weeks. It too, needs a helper/subject situation. The aim of this step is to maintain the sense of the body letting-go of unnecessary tension, and learning to hold it while being active physically. In this stage we start from a standing position. The subject at first closes their eyes and the helper moves their arms as in the previous exercise, while the subject relaxes. This is simply to re-activate the sense of 'allowing' in this new position. To stand, the subject needs enough strength and tension in the body to maintain posture. Yet many muscles need not work, so can be relaxed.

As in the previous exercise, it is best if you as the teacher, demonstrate this to the class before asking them to pair off. Take a firm hold on the subject's shoulders and move the whole body forward and backward slowly. As this is being done have the subject be aware of how their body feels, and how it responds to the movement. Make the movement a few times, making sure the subject can trust you to move them without dropping them. They need only go about four inches or so in either direction. What will probably happen is that the subject will hinge from the ankles, and their body will move back and forth rather plank-like. If this is so, have the subject be aware of it, and that if it were not for your firm grip, they would have fallen backwards or forwards.

What is done from here on needs to be approached slowly and carefully. The subject needs to be told that you are now going to move them again, but this time they should be aware that their body is plank-like because of the habitual tensions locking their muscles. After this you are going to work together to learn a new habit in standing and moving.

To do this ask the person to be aware of their behind and imagine it capable of easy movement backwards, hinging with their legs. To test whether they can manage this, take a firm hold on the shoulders, (i.e. hold the upper arms], and press gently downwards and slightly forwards. If the pelvis is still locked they will remain plank-like. If the pelvis now begins to relax, the behind will move backwards as the shoulders are pressed down and forwards. Explain to the subject that they need to have a feeling which allows them to respond to being moved, but springs their body gently back into its own upright posture when any pressure is removed. So it is a feeling of balanced yet sensitive poise. If the subject finds it hard to let go of the tensions holding their pelvis rigid, place your hand on their behind to bring awareness to that area, and have them push backwards with their behind towards your hand, while letting the shoulders and head go forwards.

Practice this and then try the same thing with the knees. Ask the subject to have the feeling that their knees are fastened to the pelvis by elastic – the muscles are elastic.

Let them imagine that the knees can easily move forward and spring back into place because of this elastic. To test this push downwards on the shoulders. It might be that they remain rigid; their knees bend but their pelvis locks again; or pelvis and knees now begin to respond easily. Perhaps when pushed down they stay down because they cannot, at the same time, keep the feeling of being like a blade of grass that bends in the wind, but springs unpright as soon as the wind stops. This is a part of learning the body skill of 'allowing' while the body is moving. So have the class practice until this skill begins to emerge. Do not expect it to become well established in one session. It will need a number of practice sessions to learn this new habit. To begin with it is enough to press the shoulders down then release, so the subject can learn to let the body maintain its own centre of gravity and balance, yet respond by squatting down and rising up again. When this is fairly well established, then start taking the subject into more complex movements. Take them forwards until they walk, then down, twist and up; backwards, sideways, down and twist, and so on until it is like an easy flowing dance. The helper, or you as the teacher, lead the dance, and the subject finds a body feeling which allows them to easily follow direction with eyes open or closed.

In order to accomplish this the subject has to learn to maintain the same sort of body feeling while lying down and allowing their arms to be moved. Bringing this into movement begins to link it with everyday activities. This is where it becomes a much more dynamic tool in teaching coex and relaxation than when the subject simply learns to relax while prone and inert. They may not otherwise bridge the gap between the open 'allowing' state and their daily actions.

As with the other lessons, this is most helpful if practised for several weeks. It thereby establishes the new body skill being learnt. It is worthwhile helping the members of the class do this by having them maintain the open state while they are no longer directed by their helper. This can be taught in a future class as below.

4 The subject now has to take what their helper enabled them to define and use it alone in their own self directed movements. Help them to do this by starting with something simple. While they are standing, ask the class to created the open state, and while maintaining it take a few steps forward. Tell them to start again if they lose the body sense of 'allowing'. Ask them to take particular notice of face, chest, and anal/genital areas. These are where tensions often show. In the face it is felt as a tense or false expression. In the chest it is experienced as holding the breath or restraining it in some way. In the anal/genital area it is felt as a tense closing up. In this last area awareness can be increased by tensing the area and then dropping the tension.

Do not be surprised if members of the class find it difficult to perform simple movements such as walking with the awareness they have been learning. It is quite normal for people to stumble or falter in just taking a step forward while they maintain the open state. The class should be allowed time to gradually develop past this stumbling point to a surer more pleasurable movement. When they can maintain the open state reasonably well while walking, try more varied movements. Let them practice until it becomes easier. If necessary, let them work with the helper again to re-define the experience of the open state. Depending upon the main structure of the class, it can be used during dancing, exercise, etc. In using it in this way, create the open state and let it's pleasure flow into the very exertion needed. Keep the genitals, face and chest open even though a lot of muscles are being used. As people feel the pleasure of moving in this way, allow the good feeling to flow with the breath. What is meant by this is that the open state causes a gentle pleasure to be felt in oneself, even in a strenuous posture or movement. When there is awareness of this pleasure let the in-breath enhance it, almost as if one were breathing-in pleasure. Then let that feeling permeate the body.

Daring to be free and the fear of being Oneself

I believe that the single most difficult aspect of teaching coex is that if offers a person freedom. Teaching how to create the 'open' state is comparatively easy. One is telling the person or class just what to do, and giving them easy to follow steps. When it comes to exploring their own spontaneous movement, however, many people pull back. They face the freedom of decision, but also they face the unknown. If you give the whole class a particular movement to do – even if quite a funny one – everyone is doing it, so the end result and performance do not matter. But if a person has to rely on themselves for creative expression, they may not remain unselfconscious. They wonder whether what they do will be RIGHT? After all, no end goal or model has been set, so what they do may not be acceptable. How are they to find out without risking expressing themselves? Most of our pupil/teacher relationship is based on copying or repeating what the teacher does or says.

I find it helpful to use one of the movements described in chapter three to begin the exploration of coex. This can be practised without using the helper/subject situation. Each person should stand in their own space, preferably on a carpet or mat. Ask them to create the open state in themselves, and carry it into the movement where the head and arms are taken slightly backwards on the in-breath, and the body taken into a squatting position on the out-breath. Ask them to repeat the movement a few times to familiarise themselves with it. When they have done this, lead them into being aware of the difference in feeling between the 'up' position and the 'down'.

The 'down' and 'up' are opposite poles of how we express ourselves not only physically but psychologically. The down expresses sleep, rest, withdrawal and non-involvement. The up expresses activity, involvement and confrontation. When we emerge from the womb, our being is confronted by a different world. In the womb there was little change. There was no otherness such as other objects or people to deal with. There was no need to reach out for ones needs because food came automatically. In life outside the womb, food does not come automatically, certainly not as we mature. There are other people and objects to deal with. Change is occuring all the time. If as a baby we found no comfort or love when we were born, it could be that we did not develop any urge to adapt to this new life. Perhaps we did not want to be involved in its change, its opposites, its necessity to find our own needs and to cope with other people. We may have wished to stay in the womb condition because there was no reward in emerging from it. So although our body matures, we might not have develped into an outgoing explorative person. With those feelings some people might 'drop out', or withdraw into alcoholism. In milder forms we might be quiet and unexpressive, not wishing to be involved in what is going on around us. The squat posture is expressive of this type of non involvement with the exterior world. But of course there is another side to withdrawal – it is also an aspect of a healthy life. If we do not honour our healthy need to sleep, to have times of privacy or cycles of lessened outer expression, then we suffer stress. So the squat also represents our ability to rest and to allow ourselves the attainment of relaxed, non-active pleasurable feelings. This could be called our 'warm comfortable place'.

The standing position expresses our involvement in the exterior world of change, opposites, and needs which require expenditure of effort. It would be ideal if each of us could move easily between these antipodes of our being. We tend to have a greater ease in one or the other though, and this is expressed in our feeling sense of each posture. It is because of this the postures can be used as an introduction to coex. Through the posture the class can be led to awareness of the feeling sense. Then from that they can learn to allow their unconscious to express what relationship they have with being down or up.

So, from having the class be aware of the difference they feel between standing and squatting, now say something like: "Now that you have become familiar with the movement, and have noticed the difference between being down and up, I would like to hear how you describe that difference."

Feeling Low – Feeling High

At this point give people a chance to say what they have experienced, without necessarily asking everyone to talk. Then say:

Okay, we are now going to continue the exercise a little further. When I suggested you do the movement, you were going up and down because you were willing to follow my instructions. Having accepted what I asked you, the movements you made were partly automatic. What I want you to do now is to discover how your feelings respond to the movement. Some of you described feeling more comfortable while down, and some of you preferred to be up. These preferences are part of the way your feelings react to everyday life, often unconsciously. What we are going to do is to honour those feelings and find out what they are telling you. So start from the standing posture, go down into the squat, and this time, if you feel no impulse to get up, stay down. Follow the impulse with your body. In other words, if you feel like going right down onto the floor, do so. It might be that during the time of the exercise, to which we are going to give ten/twenty minutes, you will not feel any feelings to get up at all, in which case stay with whatever position or movement your impulse leads you to. It might be that your feeling changes, and after a while you have an urge to stand. Or perhaps you do not have a nice feeling about being down, and have an impulse to stand right away. Therefore, think of what we are doing as an exercise in being aware of, and expressing your subtle feelings. This is helpful because often we automatically do things without having the full backing of our feelings, and this causes some degree of tension or conflict. In listening to our feelings and giving them an opportunity to express themselves we are reducing the tension, and also learning what our feeling-needs are. Give yourself time now, to explore what you feel about standing and going down.

Each person will have their own personal reaction to this exercise. In general there are three basics: [A] Not wanting to stand. [B] Not wanting to go down. [C] Moving reasonably well between the opposites.

At the end of the exercise, let people say what they felt. Whatever it is, it will almost certainly be relevant to their own situation in life. This is important, so do not think this is merely a loosening up exercise. The process of coex can be expressed through this method very capably, and although it is gentle, what people meet is a part of their own healing and self-regulatory activity. At a recent workshop one man found his feelings led him to a rather tense standing position. It seemed to express an attempt to avoid going down. It turned out that he had experienced a loss of self confidence which he had only recently moved out of, and he was anxious that he might drop back into it. The exercise showed, however, that his anxiety was causing tension, which he needed to move beyond.

A woman in the workshop felt loath to get up. It felt to her as if standing would require a great deal of strength, even aggression. This expressed her sense of difficulty in expressing herself as a woman, and her feeling of being in competition with men.

Just these two examples show that the person was facing important issues in their life. This approach to coex can be an available avenue for many people to meet and resolve such difficult feeling areas and aspects of their growth as a person. It does not need high intellectual attainment to be of real service in helping them toward such resolution. But it does need the strength of the teacher's support and their skill in creating an environment where such healing can take place. The notes already given on creative listening should be carefully read. Also, the exercise should be used in an alternating manner. What is meant by that is, after using the exercise the person should be given an opportunity to discuss the connection between what they experienced during the exercise and its link with their everyday life. The aim is not to find answers to the persons life situation but to bring greater awareness to it.

The Earth the Seed and the Sun

If you are teaching an individual or group and the time factor is not restricted, it is beneficial to use the Seed, Earth, Water and Sun meditations as exercises. There is a lot to gain from them in the way of discovering expressive body movements and creativity. Their use is described quite fully in chapter two. If you are teaching a group, you obviously need to set the mood, have participants find sufficient space, and especially, to realise they have a period of time in which they have the luxury of listening to their own being.

Awareness Transforms

When we bring awareness to any area of ourselves, whether that is to do with the way we walk, or how we feel about work or love, the quality of what is looked at changes. A woman, Hanna, felt depressed and trapped by her work situation. She had agreed with a friend to become a business partner producing baskets. After a period of time she felt unhappy, but could not determine why. She gave time to be aware of her feelings and ideas about what was happening however, and saw that she had lost her enthusiasm to run the business, but held-on-in because she believed she would be letting her partner down by leaving. It became obvious in her self consideration though, that her partner could easily manage the business if the break was planned carefully. Hanna in fact was trapped by her own feelings of what people would think of her if she went back on her agreement. Seeing this enabled her to easily make the changes she wanted. Awareness had transformed the way she SAW the situation, and so enabled her to approach it differently.

In teaching people the process of coex, it is helpful to remember that its two most frequent actions are that it expands awareness and it expresses the habitual ways our energy flows. Our awareness penetrates areas of our feeling and motivation which usually remain unconscious. When these parts of our being become known we can relate to them in a way we could not when they were unknown. Although this is a simple process in itself it is very effective. It also faces one with experience which needs perseverance and strength to meet.

This might be clearer if we understand that tension is most often a defensive or protective reaction. In taking an open allowing feeling state we temporarily drop our protective tensions. Supposing we are in an open condition while in a room with several people, one of whom we would like to get near and embrace. Usually such an urge would be suppressed if it were felt to be in disagreement with 'proper' social action. Or it might be channelled through learnt social responses toward some level of satisfaction. Perhaps we had previously been deeply hurt in openly expressing our affection as a child. So the urge to embrace could have social conditioning and also pain attached to it. Therefore, if we create an 'allowing' state, our spontaneous feelings are free to move toward being felt by us consciously. But because conditioning and pain may be attached to them, these are the first things which are felt by us.

In helping someone to become free of such conditioning and pain, there is no need to erect goals such as 'curing' or 'healing' the person. The aim is to help them achieve awareness in a way that will transform them. They need the encouragement and support to feel that meeting any conditioning and pain encountered in the process of gaining awareness, is transformative rather than threatening.

Standing and Walking

If we realise that 'standing up' means more than simply straightening ones legs, we gain an insight into what can be achieved through the use of the squatting and standing exercise. In this, standing means that from the introverted experience of babyhood we have gradually exteriorised ourselves more fully, and developed a reasonable degree of confidence about our own identity in contact with others. This confidence and exteriorisation may have met difficulties or points of crisis in its growth. So although we can stand up well physically, as a psychological or feeling person we may not be standing very high or straight. A man who is confident in a pub, may be shy and withdrawn in a dancehall. A woman who is sure of herself with her children may feel inferior and inefficient in a business.

When we give awareness to whether we have any motivation to stand, we are looking at this subtler side of our nature and observing how much inner strength is behind our act of physical standing. In one workshop a young man who had never done the exercise before found that he had no impulse at all to stand. In fact when he moved toward rising he felt threatened. On talking this out with him he said that expressing himself in everyday life was always a great struggle. He as a person never really 'stood up'. The reason for this we discovered to be that his social and family training had not taken account of how he felt and his own impulses. His parents expected him to act in certain ways whether he wished to or not, and whether he was frightened or not. So he had developed an inner attitude of doing things automatically, without any enthusiasm or creative feeling. To help this man we told him that he was now in an unusual environment where his feeling self had time to explore the act of standing. He was encouraged to express what the feeling part of him wanted to do without criticism or should's and should not's being imposed. Thus a direct communication with his 'withdrawn' feeling-self commenced. It was made plain that the enthusiasm and support of his feelings were needed in everyday life. Without them the man had felt inwardly weak. But this time the feeling self was allowed time to 'sniff out' its environment like any natural creature does before it feels sure of its ground.

Slowly and cautiously the man stood. He wept because he had never stood up in that way before. But in that first session, that was as far as he wished to go. It was sufficient for him to have stood up – anything further needed to come slowly.

This gives an idea how to work with this technique. The person must be allowed to remain at any level with which they feel comfortable. Here again, awareness transforms. Although they may find themselves stuck in some level of withdrawal, it is sufficient for them to remain in that feeling with awareness for it to gradually change. The dialogue between the feeling self and the adult/social self helps this, but transformation can arise from awareness alone.

If the person manages to stand with a good feeling of motivation and enthusiasm, then they can try LEADING THOSE FEELINGS INTO THE ACT OF WALKING. The same ways of working apply to this as to the standing.

The Seed Group

If you are working with a group of people who are explorative in their relationship with coex, the seed group structure is an excellent one to take them further. It allows aspects of self regulation which might not surface outside a group interaction. As the teacher though, it is important that you experience both types of role offered by the seed group. That is, being the central character as the seed, and being a supportive helper. Use of the seed group is described in chapter two.

Daring to be Yourself

When we allow our deepest feelings and insight to be expressed consciously, we are daring to be ourselves more fully than usual. The meeting between our deeply unconscious drives and wisdom and our waking personality makes of us a different sort of human being. True we are not unique in linking these two divergent aspects of ourselves. There are many other men and women who have done so in varying degrees. Nevertheless, the numbers are comparatively few, and it IS a new human development. When teaching it we are helping the pupil learn and explore a new human experience.

If you have led someone through the exercises given so far, they are now ready to use coex without the structure given by the squatting and standing technique. The methods already described in chapter two can be used to do this. Also, using coex to deal with particular questions is an approach appreciated by most people.

To summarise:

1 TENSING AND RELAXING ARMS. This is principally for helping people new to coex to learn how to relate to their being in an 'allowing' and 'open' manner. It gives them the experience of letting go and of spontaneous movement. Also, in working with a partner a feedback situation is developed in which the person can discover areas of tension previously unknown. Although this is a helpful place to start when teaching, the techniques used actually have a wider application than a starting point for coex. They form an excellent series of exercises which can be used to learn fuller relaxation in everyday life.

2 SQUATTING AND STANDING. I sometimes call this 'standing and walking' because it leads to walking with greater motivation. This is a structured approach to coex. The action of coex arises fairly easily within it, especially if the practitioner has already practised preparatory exercises in regard to their feeling sense and the open state. However, it can be used by itself to help the practitioner to find greater motivation and pleasure.

3 THE SEED, EARTH, WATER AND SUN. These are exercises in structured coex, and are very useful and gentle. They are adaptable for use in such environments as a yoga class; as a form of moving meditation; or as a form of relaxation in exercise classes. Children could helpfully use them in drama study, or in creative self expression.

4 THE SEED GROUP. Outside an unstructured approach to coex, this is the most powerful environment for the experience of coex's possibilities. It has so many facets it is difficult to summaries them. It is a situation in which a beginner can gently allow the very minimal level of their self regulatory experience to surface. It can be almost an experience of playing. It creates a social environment in which body contact and varied aspects of relationship can be explored in a way not usually available. For many people the caring quality of the seed group allows them expression of feelings which in todays world are often repressed. Because of the support and contact in the group, the self-regulatory process surfaces with a strength seldom found in other techniques. This form of working is so multifaceted, it can be used weekly over a period of time without going stale.

5 UNSTRUCTURED COEX. This is the simplest format, and certainly the most available in terms of where, how and when it can be used. Nevertheless, because of its simplicity it is unacceptable to people who need boundaries and directions to feel safe. Because of this, if the unstructured practice is approached too quickly, some people will act-out a self-regulatory activity to comply with the needs of the situation. To do nothing and wait, to be patient with ones own internal creative process is not a quality highly developed in many personalities in todays world.

The unstructured approach does open the door for areas of inner experience which one does not have a concept for, or expectation of, because they are outside ones present awareness. Leaving oneself open, without expectation and concept therefore heightens the possibility that new aspects of our being can express themselves.

CHAPTER 7

Individual and Social Implications

In this present century there has been an explosion in the number of people who have in some way explored their inner world. This was partly due to the discovery and public use of L.S.D., but also because of other factors. Millions of people who had never used a consciousness-changing drug started meditating, or practising yoga, or became involved in group activities such as co-counselling, the growth movement and modern psychotherapy. All of these have introduced people to other viewpoints regarding life, sex, work, society and death, than given them by parents and the society they grew up in. When such a number of people realise there are many ways of dealing with the world, there cannot help but be social and individual implications.

Because the process of coex, connecting as it does with the self-regulatory and self revealing activities in individuals, is fundamental to the practises and changes mentioned above, I see coex as central to the change. If this is understood, the birth of the changes working in the world at the moment can be assisted more easily. If not, there can only be added conflict with the forces pressing for recognition from within countless individuals.

I believe it is clear from what has already been described that through conscious cooperation with coex, the conscious personality can receive and integrate experience from what are usually unconscious life processes. For consciousness to take light into what had been the dark night of inner life process, is akin to the discovery of a completely new culture or civilised race. Just as the contact between Japan and the Western world in the last hundred years has produced radical change, so this is happening through the unveiling of the strange inner world of humanity. The similarity is quite inclusive. Just as the inter-flow between East and West has occurred despite the fact that comparatively few Easterners have been to the West, and few from the West travelled to the East, nevertheless the interchange of culture and commerce is immense. So too, although comparatively few have made any extensive exploration and study of their inner world, the few that have are influential. Many of the new attitudes in women, and new ideas and urges in regard to world politics, religion, family life, music and art, have arisen originally in a few individuals who found a creative relationship with their own inner life. They were able to see through the contricting views and standards in which they were raised. Their own inner frustration and pain demanded to be heard and they listened. Out of that arose the new themes we can now see in the theatre, films, music and social reform.

Perhaps the major point of these changes is the swing from a relationship with the world and an evaluation of it based on objective and exterior observation – such as through the microscope and telescope – to one reached through subjective inner experience – such as through intuition, feelings, imagery and dreams. While talking with me recently, the poetess Joan Ruvinsky told me of her own experience of this move from one world view to another. She was raised in a family dominated by her father's scientific work with time and the quartz crystal. Her early work was overshadowed by the standards of experimental science until her own inner life shouted to her for acknowledgement. She listened to it, noted its theme, accepted its validity, then promptly forgot it again for some years. To move from one paradigm to another is not easy. Joan is still exploring and evaluating, and in this she is representative of many of us.

For many Westerners there is a profound temptation, when the urgent call of their inner life is first felt, to leave the rational and scientific world entirely. Often they associate with an Eastern religion or guru, or try to drop their entire occidental identity. Fortunately this cannot be done in a satisfying way. The positive elements of ones own culture come knocking on the door of awareness to be included. The rational, questioning, scientific and experimental aspects of our Western identity have a great deal to offer to the unfocused, intuitive, evolutionary drive of the unconscious. Also much of the structure of our inner world is focused around the cultural symbols of Christianity and Western literature art and music. Nevertheless, because the West has entered and in some ways raped the East, it has opened itself to a cultural back flow. We can no longer live in splendid cultural isolation. Our psyche is faced with the integration not only of the Cross and the microscope, but also the Void of the East. In fact we are faced externally, and within ourself, with otherness.

I was born in 1937 from parents of different cultural backgrounds. My mother's maiden name was Banning. She grew up in Amersham, a small town in Buckinghamshire, having an English, protestant background. My father's name was Alfredo Criscuolo. He was born in London from two Italian parents. When christened I was initiated into the Catholic Church, and, to be on the safe side, the Church of England as well.

Although not an avid follower of astrology, I believe it evident that the time, place and circumstances of our birth are powerfully imprinted on us. Arriving as I did three years before the greatest international conflict the world has yet seen, and with the name of Criscuolo, I was placed in a particular relationship with people around me. Italy joining forces with Germany against the allies caused me to be treated by some as an alien and an enemy. At three however, I posed little threat even to our local Home Guard.

At that early age I had no clear concept of war or international politics. The turmoil of war around me was beyond my ken. What was a part of my understandable experience however, was the intolerances, judgements and persecutions which came from having the name Criscuolo. I remember being stood in front of the whole assembled school without any pre-warning. It was then announced that I, Anthony Thomas Criscuolo, because my parents had decided to change our name, would from that time forward be known as Anthony Crisp. I had not realised until then that a name could be a problem. For some time afterwards though, the ring of voices followed me at playtime shouting Criscuoly-oly-oly. Also, while myself and other children were running behind a horse-drawn farm cart going to the harvest field, I was hit in the face with a horse whip by the farmer – who lived three houses away from myself – and accused of being a 'little Mussolini'. I did not know at that time PRECISELY what that meant, but I got the general idea.

Compared with the treatment received by many people who, for one reason or another, are not considered as belonging to the dominant group, what happened to me was mild. Even so, such experiences left their mark. The effect became noticeable during my adolescence when I unconsciously felt alienated from the structure and attitudes of the country in which I was born and lived. The morals and goals of Britons, individually and collectively seemed strange to me. In many ways I was a stranger to the land of my birth, feeling sometimes like an Italian Roman Catholic living abroad.

With an alteration of details, the overall plot of my story is also true for a huge number of people living in the U.K. today. The number is so large it brings threat of national splintering to the point where it needs recognition. It produces a situation where the efforts of many peoples lives are other than toward a national cooperation. The problem is not simply one of foreigners or children of foreigners living in Britain. Alienation occurs beyond those boundaries today. In a country where the child of parents whose identity largely arose out of a lifetime of work, cannot obtain work, a sense of alienation and identity crisis can arise. It can occur between child and family, and child and society. The development of rapid international business activity and travel also places us regularly in direct confrontation with aliens.

In 1983 I visited Belfast and Israel for the first time. The open aggression and carrying of arms forced me to face the potentially lethal effects of alienation. In Belfast I saw whole groups of people housed within strong wire mesh cages. In Israel I witnessed Israeli holiday-makers, complete with cameras, shorts and knapsacks, carrying automatic weapons. The guns, the fought over boundaries and the stout wire mesh cages, appear to me to arise out of the same sources as my own sense of alienation – religious and political differences, anger and fears, and nationalism. When I look at Belfast and the Middle East, the message I read from the situations seems very clear. It is that if human beings are not capable of transcending the hurts and attitudes their birth environment has imprinted on them, conflict and alienation, with their consequences of international conflict, are impossible to avoid. Looking back with the wisdom of hindsight over the past twenty years, I can see that the urge to such transcendence has been the motivation to much that has happened in the Western World and in my own life.

Many people wish to transcend the barriers of personality and nationality which create for them conflict individually and socially. Millions have been attracted to organisations which appear to offer this. In fact, in the West we have seen the development of what can be called 'supermarkets for transcendence'. But if I read my own condition rightly, and recognise the need of others like me, such organisations have been inadequate flirtations with a huge need. They have been too Oriental, too centred on the charisma of the leader, and catering to the uncertainty and fear in people, which looks for an apparently divinely inspired leader who knows the 'truth' and offers certainty in the midst of uncertain change.

One can liken this to a sort of ballooning. The person who aspires to transcend their imprinted limitations rises above them. The sixties and seventies saw the spiritual sky full of transcendental balloonists who had escaped the limited moorings of their British phlegm. Their boundaries of nationality, even of sexuality, had been transcended, but to what purpose? This led to an epidemic of people who had found liberation from the limitations of their native religion, but who dived into the nearest unfamiliar one. Thousands became Moslems, Sanyasins or Buddhists – achieving a new set of prejudices and means of alienation.

Many of us are capable of stepping outside the anxieties and tensions which lead us to draw guns on each other. But it is a skill which needs to be learnt, just like walking. Perhaps it is time we began to learn, and to recognise the need for a home centred programme of education in a the art of transcending. To be able to do this well we need an understanding both of the urge to transcend, and of the forces with which we are working.

Observing the action of coex in many people, I believe it has rather an organic way of functioning. It is like a plant which takes the varied minerals surrounding it, and through its living process transforms them into its own integrated being. The plant does not become the mineral. Neither is it shaped by the forms of what it takes up. It is influenced, it is coloured, but its process transforms. The healthy human being can do likewise. A major part of unconscious mental process is to do with taking experience and integrating it into a meaningful whole. If we could trace how the development of such mental activity arose, we might find that it is a reappearance at another level of the process of digestion and absorption. But events need to be experienced to become integrated. We are an enormously sensitive and responsive living process. Our whole being can respond to what we experience or learn – words too have tremendous power within us. Often, however, we have unconsciously deadened our emotions and sensitivities, and we do not therefore properly 'take in' what we have experienced. Sam, working in a hotel as a cook, describes an experience which illustrates this point.

I had worked in the hotel for some years during the holiday season, and so was used to the crowds of people on the streets. In the middle of last season though, after having practised coex for some time, I walked out onto the street after work one day and felt a rush of fear. People thronged the pavements in such numbers many spilled off into the road. They were of all ages, all sizes and all conditions. Not only fat and thin, but occasional cripples and mentally retarted or mongoloid people too. I thought to myself, 'My God! It's all too much. I'm just a helpless ant in the midst of all these other ants'.

From that time on, although I had lived in London for many years, I began to feel fear on the streets. I was aware of the aggression, the loneliness, the broken spirit, the joy in people, and it produced feelings in me I had never experienced before. Through the use of coex I gradually saw I had felt all these things as a child con-

fronted by the world, but I had unconsciously suppressed the experience. The examples given by adults
was that feeling responses to life were out of place and
infantile. But life in London had confronted me with
people dying of cancer; T.B. was rife at that time too;
prostitutes openly walked the streets; I was often accosted
by homosexuals as a child; and instead of allowing
myself to feel the enormity of what it said about human
beings, I had shut the pain and wonder of it out. Now,
as I began to feel this through opening up in coex, it first
spoke to me as fear. Since then it has spoken in different
voices.

The voice Sam is talking about is that of his own living
being as it learns through direct experience. It is the voice
of his own learning process as it picks up real knowledge,
not from books, but out on the street, in the midst of his
family life, at the death of his dog, while washing his
mothers back in the bath and seeing her naked, and as life
itself being born and living within the whole amazing
condition of humanity and this planet. What Sam learnt is
explained in these further comments.

What I find is a big boost is that I was thrown out of
school, bottom of my class in most subjects, yet I discover inside myself the most amazing form of intelligence and vision. It seems to me from what I have been
experiencing in coex, that part of me is like a computer.
All the things my senses and emotions have experienced
are carefully recorded and then scanned for information.
Practising coex is a way of listening to what the computer has gathered from all the experience. Some of that
is very much about me personally, but a lot of it is about
life in general, and even political and religious issues. So
what I learn in this way makes me even more unique as a
person because no one else, nothing else in the universe,
has experienced or seen things quite from the time, place
and situation that I have. But also I learn things that are
universal, that are general to everybody, and enable me
to see how much a part of everything else I am.
    To be more specific – because I grew up in a world
with many prostitutes and homosexuals something happened inside myself which I was completely un-aware

of until I listened to this inner information. The scanning process saw what a huge percentage of people were manipulated through their sexual urge. Put rather crudely it was similar to the way humans trap animals or farm them. We know that if we put food in a trap an animal will be led into it by its urge to eat. We know that if we put a ram with the sheep, they will mate. Sexual hunger can be used to get people to part with their money, or to lead them where you want them to go. I recognised those things from the many bits of experience scanned, but I didn't have the courage to listen to what I had inwardly learnt until recently. On listening I saw how, deep inside, I had decided to discipline my sexuality so I would not be so easily manipulated. That unconscious decision influenced whole areas of how I developed relationships, yet I hadn't even known I had made such a decision.

What may be even more important is that out of that scanning, realisations about the social conditions in the country I live in had also been formed. For instance, what attitudes within us create prostitution anyway, and what leads us to manipulate each other? When we are so manipulated, often en-masse by political and commercial forces, why do we remain so sheep-like and follow? When we do that we are like cattle, having no self awareness at all. What sexual and social codes have we adopted, or been led to adopt through the manipulation by church and state, that place us in this sleep-like condition in which we can be farmed by people shrewd enough to do it? As far as I am concerned one of the major reasons is that WE HAVEN'T GOT GUTS ENOUGH TO LOOK AT WHAT IS HAPPENING TO US. We prefer to remain unconscious, and so avoid feeling the heightened emotions which allow us insight into ourselves and the world. We are far too busy congratulating ourselves on how well we are doing; how stupid the other person is, to really see who we are, and what the world around us is doing. And, quite frankly, that's just the way the manipulators want it. I personally want to wake up. I want to increase the understanding I have gained about myself and my environment, even if it hurts or shocks me sometimes. It is the most exciting and adventurous thing that has ever happened to me, and I'm certainly not going to give it up.

Sam is talking about awareness. He is also showing how awareness transformed his view of himself and his world. The insights which arise for Sam and others who work with the process of coex are not limited to sex, politics and manipulation. They cover every aspect of human activity and speculation, but are particularly concerned with human life, and the relationship we have with each other and the cosmos. To give an idea of the range and depth of these experiences I will quote some of them and summarise others.

Life Before Birth

As the experience deepened I realised I was knowing myself as I was before birth. No, even that is wrong. At first it seemed as if it was prior to conception. The world before conception was one in which I didn't have any sense of myself at all, so is difficult to describe. Yet I was aware of many different types of energy, each with its own very different character, and each doing its own thing quite without concern for anything else. It may sound strange, but it reminded me in some odd way of the world described in Lord of The Rings. When things moved on to me being an unborn baby, some sort of decision had been made. I felt this strongly, although even at the time I felt what an odd thing it was. Nevertheless, it seemed as if the decision had entered my own little life, on a direction or track of development which I realised was my body and its growth. I don't know if babies can be infected in the womb, but at one point I had the powerful experience of being attacked. I felt like a tree attacked by caterpillars. I don't mean I thought I was a tree. As an unborn baby I had no conception of myself. I experienced myself simply as a living organism, a separate thing which was threatened by some other life form. It seemed as if the waters I was in dealt with the infection though. But when I came out of the experience I cried with the shock of the attack. (Abie C.)

Freud, Jung and Reich have all attested to the importance and validity of psychic or subjective experience. Such
experience does not always relate to actual physical events,
but it does express the dynamics of ones inner life. In
many cases though it also expresses the truth of physical
experience. Therefore, the things that Abie and others
who have looked to their inner life tell us are important. If
we learn from them that we can raise the quality of the
way we care for unborn babies and children.

So, to summarise what I have gathered from peoples
statements about pre-birth experiences during coex, there
is awareness for unborn babies. Consciousness does not
magically start with the first breath. Nor does it have its
beginning at some particular prenatal stage of development. It seems to be a principle of life itself, always present,
but increasing in complexity and focus as the form in
which it exists develops. The unborn baby does not have
personality as we know it, but it does have a sense of existence. From this it identifies deeply with the mother and
is greatly influenced by her acceptance or rejection of it.
These responses to its situation that it feels very acutely,
become the fundamental patterns of reaction which underlie
the later development of its conscious personality. This
level of its being is also formed out of the original act of
love/sex which led to its conception. In some way that still
needs further definition, it is a triangle of the attitudes,
love, anger and blending personalities of its two parents.
But the mother particularly carries within herself, usually
without awareness, an image of maleness or femaleness,
which influences the baby – but not necessarily while still
in the womb.

Life is a Love Affair

When we remember that as baby we were in the most
intimate relationship possible with a woman – our mother
– the words love affair make sense. In no other way can
one have the intimacy of being a part of someone elses
body. As a baby we also shared the binding experience of
meeting the crisis of birth with our mother. There is also
intimacy in helplessness. Therefore, as a baby we had a
love affair with our mother. But the love may have at

times turned to all the agony, the anger, the loneliness and despair so often seen in adult love. During coex people recapture the early experience of this love affair, its wonder and its turmoil.

This love affair – our very first – cannot help but leave a deep impression on us. It will etch into us experiences which will determine the way we relate to other people for the rest of our life. Overall patterns of how we love, hate and feel began then, in our first love affair. Any inability to relate to the opposite sex, may have begun with our early love for mother or father.

Here is Mark's description of his own memories in this area.

Feelings began to arise while my wife was away, which I recognised as being connected with the time when I was put in a convalescent hospital at three years of age. My wife being away for so long had triggered the feelings into operation again, and in coex I was able to explore and deal with them.

I realised that as a three year old I had an almost instinctive emotional bond with my mother. When she allowed me to be taken from her this instinctive part of me could not understand how the very person you loved the most, and were most deeply bonded with, could let go of you. To the feelings of love inside me that was impossible. It must therefore mean, those feelings responded, that she didn't love me. This brought about two conflicting storms of emotion which although I was now realising them consciously, had influenced the way I related to women all my life. First I was murderously angry. She – my mother – might be able to cast me off without care, but I couldn't let go of her. Just being separated was therefore agony. My bond was being torn – a bond created of the deepest emotions and feelings I had – so I was being torn. And I also felt lost in timelessness. As a child I had no concept of time. I and all children live in a sense of eternity, and in that foreverness I was alone, not knowing whether the person I loved would ever come back. My pain and anger were forever.

Because this influenced the way I felt about women, it

naturally tore at my marriage. I could understand why some people murder their wife or husband when an event triggers this childhood pain and rage. Such rage attaches to the person you presently love, creating the most awful things. I was confronted by the fact that I must either – from these deepest and agonised feelings – learn to forgive my mother by seeing her as a human being trying to deal with the adult world, or my marriage was finished. For in the present situation I could not forgive my wife for going away and acting in such a way as to resurrect these murderous feelings, and this eternal agony.

By allowing the deep and previously unconscious part of me to be released and find a merging with the adult conscious part of me, I did manage to find forgiveness and understanding. It saved my marriage. It also enabled me to live with myself more easily and peacefully.

Mark has already clearly stated the social implication of his up-bringing – divorce, violence, possibly murder. He had already been divorced once. His awareness of the forces behind the break-up enabled him to prevent its repetition. The social implication of not knowing the sort of agonies and conflicts we sow in children through 'adult' behaviour, is much wider though. Mark's mother was not the only one who did not know – in her head, she knew in her heart – what lonely hospitalization would do to her child. Tens of thousand of children were hospitalized under similar conditions in the past. The result is a huge number of people who have relationship problems, sexual difficulties, and may show anti–social behaviour. If we also see that insensitive hospitalization is only one tiny aspect of what we do to children, and each of these adds up to social disorientation in some form, then difficulties in parenting can be seen as one of the fundamental causes of social and individual stress.

Sometimes I Wonder Who I Am

Whether we realise it or not each of us is born with a culturally implanted idea of who or what we are. A few hundred years ago for instance, it was commonly accepted throughout Europe that a human being was, or had the possibility of, an immortal soul. Social position also made it clear whether one was a noble or serf, master or slave. In todays world we have more of a dilemma about who and what we are. There are so many different viewpoints today, and as a group we have not dismissed the immortal soul concept, but have added some more such as the materialist view of identity beginning at birth and finishing at death. For most of us it is certainly easy to observe though, that our identity is largely relevant to our upbringing. If we were raised in China our view of life and reactions to situations would be quite different to what it would be if we were raised in Los Angeles in the U.S.A. There would be much less likelihood of our seeking a divorce as a Chinese for instance, or committing a crime.

Nevertheless, despite these marked differences in attitudes, skin colour, and even food eaten, there is a level at which we are all very similar. We all as a group reproduce sexually, we all eat and breathe, we all have a liver and a heart. Compared with our culturally imprinted self, this biological level is far older, less changeable, and more basic. When talking about our own likes and dislikes, we tend to mention clothes, music, a way of life and attitudes, yet these are all fairly superficial. Our being has more fundamental likes, dislikes and patterns of behaviour which arise from body needs and instincts. Young males the world over have a tendency to go through a period of catapults, air rifles and other means of hunting. They, along with female teenagers, have a drive to break loose from previous connections and make a life of their own, sometimes with a lot of aggression. During the use of coex, these basic drives become very apparent, and it is often noticeable how they have been repressed producing inner conflict. This repression is not only a consequence of the imprinted personality not understanding its own foundations, but also because the social world which imprinted the personality is itself in conflict with basic human drives. That social structure itself creates massive conflicts in the children and adults it is supposed to represent, is a sign of the sickness of our times. Seen in this light, some social attitudes and organisations are like a huge factory producing disturbed human beings – disturbed by city and work environments which are so foreign to deep needs that people break down. The breakdown may be in obvious ways such as mental illness, crime or physical health, but it is more frequently in subtler ways such as the inability to warmly parent children, or be a socially creative individual.

The people using the many different approaches to coex are gradually laying bare these areas of conflict in their own lives and within social organisations. Such awareness highlights the tremendous struggles and confusion that are occurring in connection with identity and its relationship with sexual drive, gender and up-bringing. Because a woman declares herself free of old sexual roles, it does not mean the deeper layer of her being will agree, and quietly withdraw its procreative drive and desire to nurture children. Because a man can be easily sterilised it does not mean he can so easily escape the natural bonding that takes place during sexual intercourse. He might escape it physically, but the living, feeling drives in him will not let him so easily escape psychically. These basic living forces in us, inseparable from consciousness, have inbuilt sexual, kinship, and self giving needs.

Beryl tells of her own discoveries about this:

After I had my second son Frank and I decided two children were enough. I felt fully in agreement with that, although it was Frank who took the step of having a vasectomy. As Brian and Eddie started school I began work again and felt a real need to become independent financially. I managed this through my work in property sales. I began to feel ill at ease physically though and thought it was stress at work. With hindsight it all seems so obvious now, but at the time I felt confused about what was happening. I remember how much pleasure I got out of having a dog and how ill I was when it died. A lot of my hair fell out.

I believe a seed was sown when my son started keeping ferrets. He had a female and when it got a year old he told me it must be mated soon or it would die. I had never known that an animal can die if it doesn't have young. Then I started attending a group practice of coex. It was another first, because I had not mixed with people who so openly talked about their inner feelings and acknowledged they were human. I realised then how hungry for that sort of companionship I had been. As my ability to use coex developed a part of myself was unveiled to view that I had never really dared accept before. I saw that I am an animal, a female one. That gives me a link with all female creatures of whatever species. I had not admittted that and had cut off in full flood my torrential drive to have children. It couldn't just neatly stop itself and do something else, and in my ignorance I didn't help it. So it built up inside like stagnant water and led to my feelings of tension and even to physical illness.

When I let that stream flow again I thought I was going to go wild for a baby. For a while I was – a week or so, but the drive gradually flowed into the way I was relating to my family and friends. I found a lot more caring and love come into the way I talked to people or felt about them. Even selling property has altered because I now have a feel for peoples personal needs in a building rather than just their business and financial needs. In a way I find hard to describe, I have also found out what religion is – it is knowing that you are connected with life itself and that it flows through you.

I believe that during this period of history humans are having to face the business of growing up and accepting responsibility for themselves and each other. The history of humankind is full of placing blame or power elsewhere. People have constantly surrounded themselves with gods and demons who directed their fate, physical well being, and even their creation. As time has gone on it has become easier to see the devils as projections of our own fears concerning our sexuality, and repressed parts of our own nature; and the gods as projections of our own latent abilities and power to create. As we recognise these angelic and demonic figures as shadows cast on the walls of our own awareness by our fear, our hopes, our transcendent beauty, and our unwillingness to accept our aloneness and creative power, we are confronted by the terrible responsibility of what we are doing to each other and the world. Despite waiting for centuries the Messiah has never come; the

Christ has not returned; the splendid space people who will banish war and want have not kept their appointments. In the end there is only you and I left, perhaps looking to the sky hoping. If we want our dreams of a Messiah or great leader to come true, then we must take over the part and live it out.

But perhaps great leaders have had their day, like the shadows of demons. Just as the hazel twig used by the dowser is lifeless and useless out of their hands, so leaders have no power except that given them by the belief and support of ordinary (?) human beings. In a vacuum leaders are as empty and without life as the twig. You and I are the Christ, the Buddha Maitreya, the expected Messiah. We are the power we give to leaders. We create each other every day. Human babies reared by animals never develop human pesonality or self awareness. We have to accept the responsibility for that too, and not avoid it by saying an unseen and mysterious God gives us being. We create human souls through our belief, our name giving, our communication with the wonder that is a baby. The visible, wonderful God called Human Beings creates other human beings. It is a miracle we are still not taking full responsibility for. When are we going to wake up to who we are?

The expanding awareness which occurs in the process of coex reveals these things. It is as if we have lived in a room and watched scenes which we took to be real, and gradually we learn how to walk into other rooms of our own house, and see the magic lanterns projecting the images. In other words we gradually become aware of our own physical and psychic functions which are responsible for the phenomena for which we blamed gods, spirits and spacemen. We see the very buttons and levers in ourselves which heal our bodies, produce happiness or depression, clarity or confusion, phantoms and gods. Not that the human personality is so godlike – far from it. But our being is itself the process of LIFE. It is the very miracle of creation bringing about human experience. God is a projection of what we are in our own being. That we have not yet fully woken up; not learnt to flex the sinews of ourselves is by the by. We are life with consciousness and a fragile sense of separateness – separateness so vulnerable it disappears in sleep, in sense deprivation, during shock, and perhaps in death.

Once we begin to recognise this action of growing awareness, of awakening, in the human soul, we can look back through past ages and see clear records of how other men and women experienced it. It is symbolised in folk-lore or spoken of directly in all cultures, and there are certain things common to these records. They nearly always include a sense of meeting something divine or transcendent. Yet it is realised that the transcendent is ones own being. The person breaks through the pains, fears and limitations of their own individual life experience and achieves a view which sees their separate life as part of an awesome process – the cosmos. This vastness, this time-less expanse, without apparent beginning or end, this careless everything, has no right or wrong in it; no up or down; no start or final destination. As humans beings we have always lived in this AMEN, but we usually keep our windows closed, a roof over our heads, the doors shut, so we are not confronted by the immensity of which we are a part. This is the Void spoken of in the East. It is the Wilderness so often mentioned in Western religion. Having no pathways, no destinations, people have created rules and regulations, destinations and beginnings to help them fend off the sense of awfulness, the feeling of aloneness, the inability to make decisions – fear! How much easier to have a God to tell us what to do and what direction to take in this directionless desert. How much less stressful than facing the infinity of choice and deciding, for no other reason than it being our wish deduced from what we are aware. "Foxes have holes, and birds have nests, but the son of man has nowhere to lay his head" (Mat. 8:20.) says the voice of mankind.

Summary

Consciousness is fundamental to the universe. We have never been without consciousness, even though our experience of it changes. In human life consciousness becomes self awareness. In this condition there is often a sense of vulnerability when confronted by the immensity of consciousness itself. In the Old Testament this is expressed by

Adam and Eve hiding when God walked in the Garden. People usually hide within veils of self deception as to who they are and of what they are capable – both in a negative and positive sense. They avoid being aware of the tragedy of human existence, but also its transcendent nature. By allowing the process of coex to expand awareness these veils are dissolved. The person then realises their aloneness, their responsibility as a co-creator, and their life in eternity.

This self-revealing which occurs with expanded awareness, allows the person to look back along the pathway of evolution – especially the evolution of consciousness. Each person holds within them the physiological and psychological record of this journey that life has made. At first it is 'unconscious', meaning it is not accessible to waking awareness. As it becomes so through expanding awareness – coex – the individual sees how, before human beings became self aware in the sense they are today, it was natural and helpful for survival to grab for oneself, to follow a leader, to have a certain type of male/female relationship. With self awareness came enormous changes in the size of groups living together, and the possibilities of relating. The patterns of domination, manipulation, grabbing for oneself, no longer worked in this new setting. In fact they led to terrible human suffering as seen in slavery, war, racial and international conflict, and political and religious manipulation. Humanity, as transcendent beings had within themselves the potential to overcome this tragedy. They intuited it and projected their wisdom onto figures known as Buddha, Christ, Krishna, etc. This is another tragedy because it abdicates responsibility and allows other human beings to manipulate, through becoming symbols, for ones own power and insight. Thus we have popes, kings, dictators and presidents.

The escalating results of this abdication from responsibility place humanity in confrontation with the threat of extinction. Despite prayers and cries for divine help, there is no other divine than that resident within ourselves. If we fail to use it to transform our old self-centred drives to ones of self giving, we are ourselves the creators of our own unhappy fate. There is an old saying that the 'truth shall set you free'. We often take it that the word 'truth' means some transcendent revelation. Perhaps some people even see it referring to a political truth such as Communism or Capitalism. We may hope that the truth is, that through some sort of therapy or process of meditation, we find our hurts healed and our problems solved, leaving us feeling GOOD. History has proven this to be an unrealistic hope. Hurts can be healed, pains can be melted, but in the end we are still left with our humanness, our vulnerability – we are still confronted with unresolved problems. If a car accident has robbed us of our legs, our healing may release the anger at our fate, allow the scream we held back as the car hit us, but we are still without legs. Despite successful therapy we are still confronted by the question of how to make love; how to get on and off buses; what we are going to do with our lives. Those questions can only be resolved by experiment and honest communication with other human beings. If I have been crippled sexually rather than physically the situation is the same. The TRUTH is our own personal humanness. Knowing and acknowledging that I am sexually crippled sets me free of it. It does this because we can only acknowledge such degrees of our own humanity by allowing love and forgiveness to be felt toward our own being and to the world around us. To love and accept oneself in this way means one has begun to accept the world AS IT IS. This love has in it the power to transcend old hurts, reach across boundaries. Maybe it would be easier if the answer to human problems were a set of rules such as a government uses. As this is not so, we will have to meet ourselves on the road to survival. Our awareness of this situation and of our own humanity is itself a point of transformation.

CHAPTER 8

Self Regulation

If the self regulatory processes of your being ceased its action you would be dead in a very short time. Even a brisk walk causes such enormous changes in the body it would kill you without the action of self regulation. The production of lactic acid, unchecked, would destroy the system. Also the drop in blood sugar, unless balanced by the release of glucose from the storage in tissues and liver, would result in collapse.

The level after level of safety factors built into our system are nothing short of incredible. For adequate functioning our blood pressure needs to be at about 110 to 120 (i.e. it displaces 110 millimetres of mercury). It can drop to 70–80 before a critical situation arises in which tissue may die because blood is not reaching it. If we lose a lot of blood, even as much as 30 or 40 percent, the self-regulatory process maintains adequate blood pressure by constricting the blood vessels. This action is controlled by a part of the brain. If that brain area is injured or destroyed, other centres take control. If they are eliminated, ganglia in the sympathetic nervous system direct the action. If they too are eliminated the walls of the arteries and veins themselves regulate their own activity.

Such functions are usually listed under the heading 'homeostasis'. The word means to 'keep level or balanced during change'. The ball cock in a toilet is an excellent example of mechanical homeostasis. As soon as we flush the toilet the ball-cock descends allowing water to pour into the cistern. When the water reaches a certain height the water entering is stopped, thus a level is maintained despite change. To quote from Anthony's *Textbook of Anatomy and Physiology* (Mosby),

The principle of homeostasis is one of the most fundamental of all physiological principles. It may be stated in this way: the body must maintain relative constancy of its chemicals and processes in order to survive. Or stated even more briefly: health ad survival depend upon the body's maintaining or quickly restoring homeostasis.

In 1885 the Belgian physiologist Leon Fredericq described it this way:

The living being is an agency of such sort that each disturbing influence induces by itself the calling forth of compensatory activity to neutralise or repair the disturbance. The higher in the scale of living beings, the more numerous, the more perfect and the more complicated do these regulatory activities become. They tend to free the organism completely from the unfavourable influences and changes occurring in the environment.

In 1900 Charles Richet a French physiologist went further by saying:

The living being is stable. It must be so in order not to be destroyed, dissolved or disintegrated by the colossal forces, often adverse, which surround it. By an apparent contradiction it maintains its stability only if it is excitable and capable of modifying itself according to external stimuli and adjusting its responses to the stimulation. In a sense it is stable because it is modifiable – the slight instability is the necessary condition for the true stability of the organism.

In 1933 Walter B. Cannon published his remarkable book *The Wisdom Of The Body* (Kegan Paul, Trench, Trubner & Co. Ltd.). Through his years of research and experiment he added enormously to the understanding of physiological homeostasis. He points out that the self-regulatory process not only has to adapt the body to outer influences, "There is also resistances to disturbance from within. For example the heat produced in maximal muscular effort, continued for twenty minutes, would be so great that, if it were not properly dissipated, it would cause some of the albuminous substances of the body to become

stiff, like a hard boiled egg". He points out that such processes are not originally given naturally, but are slowly
developed by organisms as they evolve. Thus the frog
cannot prevent free evaporation of water from its body, so
cannot be long free of its home pond. Nor can it effectively regulate its temperture, so becomes torpid and sluggish
in cold weather.

This helps in understanding what Fredericq meant in
saying the "regulatory agencies . . . free the organism completely from the unfavourable influences and changes occurring in the environment." Obviously this is only partly
true, and humans have much greater freedom from environment than the frog. Nevertheless we cannot survive in
anything except small changes of temperature, outside or
inside, but must use special equipment in, what is for us,
extreme heat and cold. Also, in the airlessness of space,
and while submerged in water, we must again use special
'clothing'. These things we create by our mental ingenuity.
Therefore, we can say that self-regulation is not a fixed
ability, and our conscious use of intelligence and experience are also aspects of the homeostatic process. Through
expanding our ability to adapt to outer and inner environments we have expanding freedom. If our ability to adapt
lessens, then our freedom lessens also.

This learning process even takes place in such major
homeostatic features as heat control and regulation of
blood sugar level. During this century it was found that
for quite a long period after birth babies have little control
of temperature regulation. When exposed to cold their
temperature drops with hardly any reaction to prevent it,
rather like a frog. There are also much greater swings in a
baby's blood sugar level than in an adult. The baby only
gradually 'learns' to respond to these new features of inner
and outer change after the steady temperature and blood
sugar of its prenatal life in the internal sea of its mother.

We could perhaps say the baby learned such regulation
unconsciously, or without conscious deliberation. In order
to gain greater 'freedom' though, even the baby is faced by
the need to learn. The unconscious wisdom which enables
it to learn complicated bodily adaptations also operates in
adults and in other ways. Walter Cannon describes this as
follows:

Many years ago Murphy and I observed with X rays a curious phenomena after the first part of the small intestine (the duodenum) had been cut across and sewed together again. Although peristaltic waves were passing routinely over the stomach, the sphincter at the outlet (the pyloric sphincter) held tight against them, and only after about five hours did it relax and permit the gastric contents to enter the injured gut. The interest here lies in the relation of the delay to the process of healing; according to surgical observation, about four hours are required after an intestinal suture for a plastic exudate to form and make a tight joint. It was after the proper time had elapsed for that process to come to completion, therefore, that the chyme from the stomach was allowed to advance. Similar results were obtained when the section and suture were made further along the alimentary canal.

Such unconscious though purposeful activities are expressions of this inner wisdom our being has, and are all part of our self-regulatory process. The urge to eat and drink, to work, play and learn, the longing to hold someone and be held, to make love; to sleep and wake, are all ways we keep the balance of our nature. If any of these are severely curtailed our nature may become unbalanced and even crippled in its ability to freely extend itself in reasonable freedom.

Caron Kent adds to the usually mentioned instincts what he sees as one of the most fundamental – the urge to grow. From conception onwards this urge is powerfully manifest. From conception until birth the growing organism increases its weight alone up to 27 million times. So it is an energetic urge, but also one which brings detailed control over the miracle of forming a living human body. This comes about by stage after stage of formative forces acting in the construction of our being. As an egg and sperm we are tiny single celled creatures. The next two stages of development as the cells increase in size and number resembles the activities found in many simple living things such as plants. The twenty day old embryo develops four branchial grooves, which in the embryo of a fish grow into gills. At this point the formative forces which produce a fish are active, as were the formative forces of a plant at an earlier stage. These are then supplanted by forces which bring about features of the mammallian upright animal we are. As one textbook states, "A human is not constructed like a modern office building, as cheaply and efficiently as possible...but rather like an ancient historic edifice to which wings and sections were added at different times and which was not modernised until it was almost completed."

If we recall Richet's statement that instability is the necessary condition for true stability, and consider how this works in the realm of the personality, we have some idea of psychological as well as physiological homeostasis. In a very simplistic sense if we are overcome by fear and feel unable to move, unless we are capable of releasing confidence we will remain paralysed. If our psyche is not 'unstable' or mobile enough, this compensatory shift cannot take place. These shifts, between the dynamic opposites of our nature – tension and relaxation; pain and pleasure; spontaneity and control, are vital for our healthy psychological survival. Factors preventing such mobility are causes for illness and even death. Locked feelings of guilt, shock or stress are recognised as productive of major illness. So part of the healthy homeostatic action is to actually be 'mobile' enough to deeply grieve or release emotion, instead of being rigidly controlled or coping. The 'control' and the 'out of control' balance each other. If we are so controlled that we become ill through suppressed anger or grief, we are less in control of our life and well being than someone who can let themselves cry uncontrollably for a while.

It is partly this ability to have a wide range of choices or opposites available to us that makes human survival and self-regulation more efficient than in other animals. In Africa for instance, herds of deer are being driven from the open grasslands because of human use of the land. The instincts of the deer lead them to always seek survival on the open plains, because this has always been their habitat. It is 'natural' for them to hide from enemies on the plain. But on the plains they are killed, and it would be better for their survival to hide in the forested areas. To manage that, however, they would have to be capable of suppressing their instinctive 'natural' drive, and acting in a new way.

Perhaps human beings faced a similar conflict in the past. When forests dwindled their only chance of survival was in open country which was an 'unnatural' habitat for them. So to survive they had to deny their instinctive inner urge. Perhaps this is where the idea of original sin arose, when humans denied the voice of God/instinct within them. However, it happened, humans can now question their own drives and evaluate them against survival and achievement. They thereby have extended their homeostatic functions. Ling and Buckman, in their book *Lysergic Acid in The Treatment of Neurosis*, say, "New areas of the brain had to be developed not only to integrate, but also to inhibit primitive survival oriented impulses and to enable them to store stimuli to act on them later. It is this ability to defer action and to act in a purposeful and objective rather than instinctive way that distinguishes the well integrated adult from the child, the primitive from the neurotic."

Ron Hubbard looked at human beings as if they were an engineering problem. Although this gives a different view from someone like Jung, it does have a lot of helpful information. Writing about the human computer, which he calls the Analyser, Hubbard describes it as capable of computing on any problem and arriving at a correct conclusion if the information it has is sound. It can work extremely quickly and can handle large numbers of problems simultaneously, as occurs when we drive a car. It can re-evaluate its past memories and conclusions, and come to new conclusions. It has a nearly infinite memory bank. It is self-determining and does not need an outside operator. It is also self-regulating and avoids, through estimating probable outcomes, future damage. Through the senses it contacts the objective world, and has a sense of self. Its memories are stored in time sequence, with full colour, movement, sound, smell, feeling, and self awareness. It has the faculty of imagination to enable it to compute on probabilities or create new survival aids. It is also portable.

Hubbard recognised that anyone with a healthy body who did not have brain damage through injury or surgery, had all the above abilities. Nevertheless, despite the fact the human computer is self-regulating, Hubbard had to admit that with all its faculties, the computer was frequently ill or malfunctioning. Experimenting with hypnosis on a patient who was colour blind and could not remember sounds or images, Hubbard found the person could be relaxed to a point where the problems disappeared. At this level the person could think clearly, had no colour blindness, had consideration for his wife, all of which were usually missing, but were again absent on the patient's return to 'normal' consciousness. So Hubbard's conclusion from this and other experiments was that underneath the functional aberrations was a whole and healthy person. This left the question though as to how the aberrations got into the computer.

Further experiment showed that any sort of aberration such as stuttering, hallucinations, phobias, compulsions, schizophrenia, fears, hysterical blindness, paralysis, could all be brought about in healthy hypnotic subjects simply by suggesting it. Such suggestions as: "When you awake you will not be able to hear/feel anything in your arm/ remember who you are. You will be sick every time you eat an apply/frightened when you get near women/etc," brought about the aberration it described. With hypnosis however, the suggested deafness or fear faded fairly quickly, simply because the 'human computer' is self-regulating. So what causes the aberrations which haunt people for years to stay in place?

Hubbard's work led him to see that the non-hypnotic aberrations get in from the outside world. The only reasons aberrations could stay in place in the human computer would be if, unlike general experience, their causative experience had got past the Analyser, could not be recalled, and so could not be re-evaluated. He gives the example of an adding machine which works perfectly unless we hold down the number seven. When the seven is held down all furture calculations are wrong. The machine then seems insane. Allow the seven up and sanity returns, just as it does when the hypnotic suggestion is removed. In his book *'Dianetics-The Evolution Of A Science'*, Hubbard explains what he discovered to be the cause of the 'held down seven'. It was PAIN. During a painful life experience such as an accident or frightening surgical operation in childhood, our analyser is knocked out of operation. A lump of experience enters us unassessed. It is not our analyser which operates when we put our hand on a hot stove, crash in a car, fall under a blow from dad, or feel the agony of mum apparently having deserted us. It is the reactive or instinctive mind.

Our memory is a full experience of sound, sight, emotions and pain! Once we have felt the pain of being burnt, next time our hand gets even near such heat an automatic action pulls our body away. The same happens with emotional pain. To pull away is reactive and seems necessary for survival. So we automatically pull away not only from painful and frightening things in the outer world, but also from any part of our inner memory and feelings which are painful or frightening. Pulling our consciousness away from a memory means we cannot recall or evaluate and integrate it. We may remember the event, but when it comes to recalling the painful emotions and fears we pull back. Therefore many areas of vitally important experience, decisions and thoughts connected with it, wisdom learned from it, are HELD DOWN SEVENS. Also, suggestions may have entered the memory at the same time. If a man is involved in a car accident, and during it someone shouts – "DON'T MOVE!", this is just as active as any hypnotic suggestion. Because it is held back from the self-regulating activity of rememberance and evaluation though, it can remain active. Therefore the man may literally not move, not take chances in life, always be worried something is going to hurt him.

Hubbard called these moments of painful un-evaluated experience 'engrams'. These not only caused aberrations in the person but were also contagious. They lead to an acting out of our pain on our children or others. A mother lost a baby and nearly died. Her pain and fear are now engrams. This leads her to irrational behaviour. So when her daughter shows affection for boyfriends mother hits or threatens her because of her own fear of pregnancy. Her daughter grows up with a fear of sex. Some such reactive behaviour is passed on for generation after generation unless it is re-evaluated. Reich called it the THE EMOTIONAL PLAGUE. War, political murder, religious carnage, social discrimination, go on through the centuries despite human ability to reason and see them as evils. As Reich says, "If you live in a cellar too long, you will hate the sunshine." There can be no real change in individual and social conditions at an emotional and feeling level unless individuals agree to re-evaluate their own unconscious pains, longings and values.

In Europe and the U.S.A. today so many babies are battered to death that infants have a high probability of being battered rather than being sick from normal causes. Also, parents who have not re-evaluated the pains of several wars have passed their aberrations to children who now are themselves raising families. This means more individual and social sickness, which in turn means more broken homes, which produces more children who will pass on their own pain.

It goes on and on. To stop it we need, as adults with egos, to learn how to extend our self-regulatory process. We need to do this with awareness of our natural avoidance of pain and fear. As Von Franz says in *Man and His Symbols,* we "must get rid of purposive and wishful aims. The ego must be able to listen."

What will happen then? The pieces of experience which had been 'held down' can be released for integration and understanding. This can only occur if we let ourselves 'experience' what is released. During reactive behaviour we are seldom coolly intellectual. Most of what occurs is deeply emotional or physical. Therefore to calmly have an intellectual view of the experience is not enough. To experience it is to feel its deeply emotional or physical quality.

Dr. Oliver Sacks worked with the drug L. Dopa with patients who had lain in a coma-like state for years. This led them to wake and once more consciously face the world of objective and subjective experience. He says of these 'awakenings' "all the operations in coming to terms with oneself and the world, in face of continual changes in both, are subsumed in Claud Bernard's fundamental concept of 'homeostasis'. . . We have to recognise homeostatic endeavours at all levels of being, from molecular and cellular to social and cultural, all in infinite relation to each other."

His patients, often severely dis-eased physically and emotionally, sometimes managed, he says, to become astute and expert navigators, steering themselves through seas of trouble which would have caused less expert patients to founder on the spot. "Thus some patients with severe illnesses got well and remained so, and some less ill never managed. They had obviously learned or not learned to work with their own nature."

He goes on to say that we must concede the possibility that nature, and, therefore, human nature, has an almost limitless ability to re-organise itself at chemical, cellular and hormonal levels. This is seen in action where, with the 'will to get well' patients inexplicably recover from the most serious of illnesses. "One must allow," he writes "with surprise, with delight, that such things happen. Health goes deeper than any disease."

Summary

- Self regulation is fundamental to all cosmic activities and life forms.
- In humans it acts both at a physical and a psychological level.
- It assures survival.
- It is partly a spontaneous process and is partly learned.
- Most self-regulation occurs unconsciously, and learning to cooperate with its action is a learnt skill.
- Such skill enlarges ones possibilities.
- Vomiting and digestion are functions of physical self-regulation.
- The rising into consciousness of emotions and experience for integration and re-evaluation are functions of psychological self-regulation.
- Pain and such feelings as fear and guilt frequently cause us to prevent experience and emotions from emerging into consciousness.
- Freud showed that if a person is afraid of sexual feelings their sexuality is repressed even in their dreams.
- Such deeply repressed feelings cause psychological and physical tension and illness.
- Allowing spontaneous body and feeling fantasy allows the emotions and experience held in the unconscious to be released, evaluated and integrated.
- At points where fear or pain usually block the process

one can decisively allow the self-regulatory process to continue.

- Because this allows previously unrealised experience to be known, an enlargement of our personal self awareness occurs.

CHAPTER 9

The History of Coex

A knowledge of history helps us have a wider and more tolerant view of ourselves and others. In connection with coex it helps us to have a more educated approach to the sort of claims made by groups such as Subud, that they have a unique power they are sharing with the world. In fact, their unique 'force' has appeared many times before in slightly different guises, but also obvious forms of coex.

Although the use of the self-regulatory forces in the human being is not new to our own times, it has waxed and waned with each culture. Each culture and period in history has also developed a slightly different theoretical explanation, and different approach. The overall change has been that the further back one looks, the more religious and symbolic the approach – the nearer we come to our own times the more empirical and rational it has been.

Even from the earliest historical times there is evidence that humans used medical and psychological skills to deal with physical and psychic disorders. Shamans, witch-doctors, priests and priestesses were the early administrators of such help. Although some of their techniques were originally judged as ineffective, the growth of psychobiological knowledge has shown them to incorporate elements of hypnosis, suggestion treatment, use of the dream process, with herbal knowledge.

Psychologists like Patricia Norris, clinical director of the Biofeedback and Psychophysiology Centre at the Meninger Foundation, are experimenting with such techniques and finding they work. Norris uses imaging or visualisation methods to help people heal serious illness such as cancer. Whether we look at shamanic or modern psychological usage, what we find is that the technique helps the patient develop a more positive inner feeling state in regard to their physical illness or fears. The self-regulatory process attempts this sort of shift itself in dreaming, and the techniques such as the dramatic rituals of shamanism, produced an environment where the coex linked dramatisation already described in other chapters could be expressed. Modern research suggests that this may actually lead the activity of the immune system to greater efficiency.

Whether we look at the approach used by the Hindus, Chinese, Celts, Red Indians, Africans or Aborigines, they were very holistic. They were aimed at producing not only physical and psychological changes, but also to bring the patient into a more satisfying relationship with their environment and their social group. In this sense they linked physical mental and spiritual aspects of the person.

Looking at the details of some of these approaches it can be seen that amongst the 'stone age' type races, most had a powerful relationship with their dream life. The energies and emotions in a dream were often given expression. This was done in a variety of ways. Sometimes they were acted out in a group drama or dance. The Seneca Indians said that the soul often has desires it has been unable to express consciously. The Hurons believed that if these hidden desires were kept unexpressed the soul might become angry, and it might revolt 'against the body, causing various diseases, and even death...' To quote from my book *Do You Dream*:

> The Indian tribes mentioned often had a sort of social psychiatry in which dreamers were allowed to live out their hidden (unconscious) desires that were threatening health and well being. Thus a dreamer would be allowed sexual freedoms with others; unlawful actions; objects desired; or feasts, etc.. Although these people as a society were usually modest and shy, and chastity and marital fidelity were public ideals.

This very direct admittance and expression of real needs is not common, either in the past or present. Most often the energies were given religious, dance, or ritualistic expression. One tribe, the Masai, come near to it however. The men form a group which shout, sing, cry, scream, dance and move to express their bottled-up feelings, fears and energy. No doubt this provides an environment for spontaneous action to erupt.

Sex and Coex in New Guinea

Michaela Denis, in her book *Leopard In My Lap*, tells of an interesting practise used by the Chimbu people of New Guinea. One of their 'dances' takes the form of the men and women sitting around the edge of a large hut. They are arranged alternately male and female, the men facing the women. With accompanying drumming they gradually draw close and the men passionately rub noses and faces with the woman on their right, then the one on their left. This carries on for a long period and with obvious pleasure and ardour. The dance seems to be a way of safely allowing the sexual feelings within a group to find expression.

In the ancient world a great many of the ways people used coex was within a religious framework. The unconscious was allowed to express within accepted symbols and boundaries. Frequently the practitioner held the belief structure that it was a god or a spirit which expressed through them. Given the manner in which the unconscious expresses itself in symbols and readily takes up and uses any available belief system, such practises still obviously remain as self regulatory. In *Man and His Symbols* Jung tells of a Hindu widow who capably directed her household and employees by going into a trance and speaking with the same confidence, voice and authority as her dead husband. After all, she had lived with him many years, and his mannerisms and attitudes were well recorded in her unconscious. By allowing her being to express itself in that way, she maintained an equilibrium which might otherwise have been difficult.

Shaktipat – The Indian Way to Enlightenment

In his article Between Coma and Convulsion, in *Energy and Character*, David Boadella quotes the report of a person studying the self-regulatory practices in India. Although this is a recent account, the yoga practice it describes has been used for many centuries in India:

I have been in India for about four months now and I thought the readers of *Energy and Character* might be interested in the similarities between Reichian work and Shaktipat or Kriya Yoga. The Sanscrit word 'shakti' means energy, bio-energy, or more correctly, bio-cosmic energy. Shaktipat is a practice which is described as the loosening of this energy by a guru from the way it may be blocked in us. When this shakti energy is loosened and no longer tightly bound by the control of the conscious mind it begins to circulate in the body. It is then said to open up energy channels or pathways, and usually begins to manifest in what are known as 'kriya'. Kriyas are spontaneous movements of the body and of the respiratory system. One interesting aspect of kriyas, which resemble Reichian abreaction, is that they very often manifest as highly involved asanas (body postures) and as mudras (meditational postures involving the hands). I have seen many persons who practice shakipat enter a phase of intense energy flow in which breathing becomes rapid and involuntary and in which people begin with great rapidity to do asanas they never knew and which they ordinarily would never have been able to perform. Although the conscious practice of asanas facilitates this process, true hatha yoga (Indian techniques using physiological processes to integrate ones being) occurs involuntarily in this kriya phase. The burst of energy that results is sometimes astounding and may continue for well over an hour. The movements in some individuals are so intense and frantic they appear dangerous. In other persons the movements are soft, delicate and flowing. Thus some persons may breathe like locomotives, beat themselves repeatedly, stand on their heads, bellow, twist their limbs in the most unbelievable postures; others begin to dance harmoniously, to sing softly in languages they have never learned, to become playful and flirtatious and to utter strange sounds.

The explanation for this is that the shakti is opening or purifying obstructions in the energy pathways, that the individual is working out the results of past actions and experience, and that an evolutionary process is allowed to unfold which eventually will result in an expansion of awareness.

In this kind of meditation the individual sits still, but not rigidly; he doesn't concentrate in any way, but simply relaxes as much as possible and permits the energy to do its thing. The energy is of course thought of as ultimately cosmic or divine. Hence the path of enlightenment lies in relinquishing ego control and indentifications and allowing this bio-cosmic energy to express itself and lead us. The final results of this process is the opening of the highest brain centres in a new type of consciousness in which the individual merges with the universal consciousness. The total process takes a very long time but this should not dissuade us as each stage has its own rewards. The bodily spasms, automatic breathing, asanas, contortions and reflex patterns that manifest spontaneously as the energy gains momentum all serve to purify the organism. Though some of these phenomena may sound strange they are not experienced as unpleasant once the practitioner no longer totally identifies with bodily processes. Thus the meditator can be totally in their body without identifying totally with its experiences.

Hallucination – or is it My Unconscious Speaking?

This very precise description shows that Shaktipat is quite clearly of the spiritualistic belief structure mentioned elsewhere. In spiritualistic trances of the stone age races and of today, similar processes to the above are being expressed, but within different boundaries and limitations. Modern day spiritualists still use this approach to the self-regulatory process of the unconscious. The unconscious has no difficulty in speaking in different 'languages', or expressing different racial types, personalities, or even animals.

In any attempt to understand the type of experiences described above, one needs to know a little about the various functions of the unconscious. The process of dream making and waking drama formation have already been covered, but one other aspect is important. It is the function which deals with body language. Humans have an ability to 'read' body language, but it usually takes place unconsciously. It was probably developed in the human race prior to the emergence of spoken language as we know it today. Now it remains as an almost unused function, but operates at times during shock or 'trance' conditions – i.e., when the conscious personality surrenders its decision making and critical faculties. Philip Zimbardo, in the tenth edition of *Psychology and Life* (Scott, Foresman & Co.), gives a fascinating example of this from his own experience. "It was my first day back to work after recovering from a traumatic automobile accident. I was lucky to be alive with only torn ligaments in my leg and a concussion: the driver had been killed by the impact of a head-on collision. As I hobbled up the three flights of stairs supported by a crutch, my initial joy of returning to school was suddenly suspended. With each step I took a strange sensation occurred: I could 'feel' myself BECOMING my younger brother, George. Not IMAGINE 'as if' I were George, but being transformed physically to be him.

I perceived my face changing to be his face and my body doing likewise. My limp became more pronounced, and it took great strength to climb the last flight. In a panic, I shut myself in my office, not wanting anyone to witness this strange transformation. I avoided looking at my reflection in the window for fear I would see his face and not mine. Had I really become my brother or was I MERELY hallucinating?

Time passed during which I tried frantically to relax, 'to pull myself together,' and make sense of my distorted sense impressions. After all, I was a normal, serious scientist type not given to such flights of fancy. I lived by the reality principle.

My secretary and colleagues knocked and came into the office before I could say I was busy. They were worried by my abrupt disappearing act. They were relieved to see I was 'my old self again,' and I was relieved to see them responding to me as if I were Phil and not George. A glance at my reflection confirmed my hope. I had changed back, 'or was no longer George ...or George was no longer manifesting himself in me.' Whatever? Weird, no? But why?

When we were children, George had infantile paralysis and for a time had to wear leg braces and walk with crutches. I would accompany him to therapy sessions and observe his frustration, embarrassment, and anger at not being able to function normally. Since we were only eighteen months apart in age, I could readily empathise with his feelings. I may have also felt guilty at being glad I too was not crippled. Once I recall volunteering to exchange places with him in the swimming pool exercises, but the nurse chided me, 'being crippled is not fun and games young man.' I was about four at the time.

As I hobbled up the stairs to my office some twenty five years later, the pattern of feedback sensory stimulation reactivated this prerecorded motor action plan. Memories of George's posture and movement were enacted. I had retained mimicry responses of his motor activity that I had observed so intensely. Now I was changing places with him, but not consciously and not volitionally. The suddenness and vividness of the hallucination was frightening because it was so real, yet at the same time contradicted my knowledge of reality.

Philip Zimbardo calls his experience an hallucination, perhaps because he felt fear. However, if we remember something we do not call it an hallucination but a memory. Realising that we remember via body feelings, posture, emotion as well as images and words, enables us to see that Philip, because he was in a similar situation to that which his brother had been, remembered a whole set of responses. During coex such experiences are not unusual. When they are not seen as abnormal we can accept them without anxiety and they add to our range of information and experience. In fact, if Philip had not been disturbed by his experience, but had sought it as a means of understanding his brother, he could have gathered a great deal of information from it. If we realise that we gather such information from everybody we contact, we can see that we have a very rich source of insight into the lives of those around us. These are important points to understand because we are looking at historical approaches to coex. They help to explain why some uses of coex, which appear fantastic or irrational to us, were in fact extremely useful in some settings.

Trances Spirit Healing and Possession

Carol Laderman, an anthropologist who went to study childbirth practices in Malaysia, found that shamanic healers, who it was thought had disappeared 75 years ago, were still an everyday part of village life, (*Science Digest* July 1983, Trances That Heal-Rites Rituals and Brain Chemicals). To study their methods she became the apprentice of Pak Long Awang, himself a traditional shamanic healer. It is interesting that although she is highly educated in Western thought, she has the same fear of the unconscious as Philip Zimbardo. She says,

> For almost two years after my arrival in the village, I refused to undergo one of the shaman's trances. Having become a member of Pak Long's entourage, I had attended healing ceremonies with growing regularity; the shaman had even adopted me as his own daughter. Still, as a Westerner and a scientist, I was afraid to enter trances – afraid I might embarrass myself or, worse, never come out at all. My reluctance became a standing joke among the villagers.

She goes on to say what some of the healing sessions she attended were like. A very fat woman for instance, who regularly experienced depression because of her awkwardness and girth, while 'entranced' by the music of drums and gongs, and Pak Long's chants, rose from her 'sleeping mat' with the grace of a lithe young girl and danced the role of the beautiful princess in the Malay Opera before a delighted audience of friends and neighbours. Afterwards her ailment disappeared.

Eventually Carol took the plunge herself.

> As the vibrations of the drums and gongs entered my body, my eyes seemed to glaze over. As the music became louder my mouth opened, trembling uncontrollably. I began to feel cold winds blowing inside my chest, winds that increased in intensity as the music swelled and accelerated until it felt as if a hurricane was raging within my heart. I put my hands on my chest to try to calm it, but instead I began to move my shoulders and then the upper part of my body as if I were about to get up and dance. With the last vestiges of my self

control, I prevented myself; I still feared embarrassment But as the music swelled to a climax I began to move my head so quickly and violently that, had I not been in trance, my neck would undoubtedly have snapped.

What Carol Laderman describes appears to be just the same sort of movements as those experienced in 'Shaktipat' and in modern coex. The approach, however, is quite different. In Shaktipat 'trance' is achieved by the individual sitting "still, but not rigidly; he does not concentrate in any way, but simply relaxes." In Malaysian shamanism, trance is entered "through cultural cues, ritual props, incantations, songs and stories. Percussive music, a steady, musical pulse." In modern coex similar states can be experienced simply by allowing spontaneous movement. So it seems as if all that is important is that the persons own fears, cultural theories and needs are respected. For instance in Haiti, the trance is often accompanied by 'possession' by the god Ghede, which is manifested by a particular physical posture.

Buddhism and the Way of Liberation

Ancient approaches to coex were not always in the form of trance or possession though. Two thousand five hundred years ago Guatama the Buddha gave an impulse to the world which has developed a quite different relationship with self regulatory processes. In terms of coex we can see these as Zen meditation. Tibetan Buddhism, the Chinese meditation described in the book *The Secret of The Golden Flower*, and Vipassana meditation. In these an open permitting state of consciousness is held. Thus the experiences described under Shaktipat may arise into consciousness. In the Buddhist tradition though, these are held back from physical expression and seen as illusory aspects of self which will pass away. As with Shaktipat and most of the older approaches, one seldom hears of people experiencing and transforming childhood experience. The direct experience of ourselves in this way is more Western than Eastern, though definitely not our exclusive property. What is noticeable in the Buddhist tradition is more of an emphasis on introversion and withdrawal from the external activity. Thus, what is discovered within is seldom used to change social structure in the way described in chapter seven. But in its essence, Buddhism does not suggest this one sidedness of retreat. And in the techniques of Zen and Vipassana, especially in their Western adaptations, a really helpful approach to coex is seen. Perhaps the most useful aspect of the training is in the opening and letting go of the ego, yet learning not to be lost in the forces and images which arise.

A very clear example of this is given in Tibetan Buddhism. Such teachings are very old. In her book *Secret Oral Teachings of Tibetan Buddhist Sects*, Alexandra David-Neal writes:

> Liberation is achieved by the practice of non-activity, say the Masters of the Secret Teachings.
>
> What is, according to them, non-activity? Let us first of all notice that it has nothing in common with the quietism of certain Christian or oriental mystics. Ought one to believe that it consists in inertia and that the disciples of the Masters who honour it are exhorted to abstain from doing anything whatever? Certainly not. In the first place it is impossible for a living being to do nothing. To exist is, in itself, a kind of activity. The doctrine of non-action does not in any way aim at those actions which are habitual in life such as eating, sleeping, walking, speaking, reading, studying, etc. In contradistinction to the Taoist mystics who, in general, consider that the practice of non-activity requires complete isolation in a hermitage, the Masters of the Secret Teachings, although prone to appreciate the 'joys of solitude', do not consider them in any way indispensable. As for the practice of non-activity itself, they judge it as absolutely necessary for the production of the state of deliverance.
>
> What then is this activity from which one ought to abstain? It is the disordered activity of the mind which, unceasingly, devotes itself to the work of a builder erecting ideas, creating an imaginary world in which it shuts itself like a chrysalis in its cocoon.

In the Buddhist meditation called Vipassana, the process of self regulation is allowed to let the flow of consciousness present ones innate images, fears, hopes and imaginings about life and death, and to recognise them for what they are – images, fears, hopes and ideas. In this way the attachment and even pain we experienced in connection with them falls away in some degree. That is liberation.

Christianity's Unwanted Secret

Another impulse more embedded in Western culture, but perhaps less accepted today, is that begun by the early Christians. This is very definitely an example of a group of people permitting the self-regulatory action to express itself consciously. It is what we call Pentecostalism, and from the point of view of coex, is in may ways similar to Shaktipat. The guru, Jesus, was the means of stimulating the release, or giving 'grace'. Because we are acquainted with the dogmas and belief structure of Christianity in some measure, we can more readily see how a natural process, self regulation, can become deified and surrounded by religious symbols and ritual. Just as the views of Buddhism and shamanism edited what aspects of the unconscious were permissible, (i.e. in Vipassana it is not acceptable to go into 'trance' or be 'possessed'. In shamanism it is thought ineffective if one only sits and remains aware of the flow of arising images) so in the Pentecostal approach, what is allowed must in some way link with Christ, God or biblical statements. Nevertheless, the 'drunkenness', speaking in 'tongues', the flow of cosmic energy – holy ghost – are all akin to Shaktipat and modern coex.

Pentecostal Christianity speaks of gifts of the spirit. These are listed as the gift of: the word of wisdom; the word of knowledge; faith healing; the working of miracles; prophecy; the discerning of spirits; diverse kinds of tongues; and interpretation of tongues.

Most of these are easily recognisable descriptions of faculties of the unconscious. The unconscious is constantly scanning information and considering the highest probable outcome – thus prophecy. Access to universal aspects of consciousness allow the gaining of insights which might also account for prophecy, wisdom and words of knowledge. Speaking in tongues is a common way in which the unconscious expresses its feelings and insights. It is a level three expression in Van Rhijn/Caldwell's levels of consciousness. When the 'tongues' are considered as symbolic expression they transform into meaningful words, just as dream symbols do. My experiments with such phenomena convincingly show the common link between these often considered unrelated phenomena and coex.

Discerning of spirits means the ability to look into a human heart and see what is hidden there. Considering how much we can learn subliminally through body language and verbal cues, this is another straightforward unconscious faculty. But imagine a group of people all 'worshipping' as is described of Pentecost, when the disciples were taken to be drunk. (Acts 1:12 to 2:13) There were 120 gathered in a room, men and women being equals – "All these with one accord devoted themselves to prayer, together with the women and Mary the mother of Jesus, and with his brothers." Considering present day Pentecostalism and other forms of coex, this large group would include people who would be shouting in tongues, others would be crying, moving their bodies, discerning spirits, and generally creating a bedlam of noise. Any newcomer to the group, not having had explained what was being attempted – that each be open to the Spirit and be moved by it – might think the people were crazy or drunk.

Saint Paul – Killer of the Spontaneous

Because of the obvious cultural fear we have regarding spontaneous expression, it is interesting to remind ourselves of what Paul said to the early Christians (Cor 1.14:26 to 40)

> ...If therefore the whole church assembles and all speak in tongues, and outsiders or unbelievers enter, will they not say you are mad?
> ...If any speak in a tongue, let there be two or at the most three, and each in turn; and let one interpret. But if there is no one to interpret let each of them keep silence in church and speak to himself and God.
> ...As in all the churches of the saints, the women should keep silence in the churches. For they are not

permitted to speak, but should be subordinate as even the law (Jewish law?) says...For it is shameful for a woman to speak in church.

Comparing the original pentecost with the church services of today, I believe it is obvious where Paul's advice, still rooted in Jewish male authoritarianism, led christianity. The church gained converts, but as for helping it to experience the calm love of life the guru who consorted with prostitutes had, Paul played the role of murderer.

Mesmer – Father of Modern Psychotherapy

Coming nearer to our own times we find a connecting link between past and present in Franz Anton Mesmer. In about the year 1775 Mesmer, a qualified doctor three times over, began to experiment with magnets. He found that patients who had previously been incurable were healed when these were placed on their bodies. For a year he had a mania for experimenting with magnets in quite extraordinary ways. But within that period he realised the same healing results could be obtained without using the magnets. He found that simply by stroking or touching the patient along the line of the nerves, the muscles would begin to twitch. This twitching, he said, should not cause alarm, even if it led, as it usually did, to an intensification of the patients symptoms or even convulsive movements. Throughout these releases, noisy and explosive though they were, he saw how patients could experience a healing of the distressing symptoms.

Prior to this time these convulsive releases were considered to be the work of devils or spirits. This attitude arose out of Christian belief, and Jesus and the disciples clearly used the same technique. In the New Testament are descriptions of people cured by these convulsive releases. Mesmer is a transforming link with our own times because his approach to this phenomena was an experimental and evaluative one. Nevertheless he was still bound to the past by his belief that another human beings prescence was necessary to act as a channel for a cosmic energy to reach the sick person. Thus he still remained, in this aspect, in connection with the guru as agent of change tradition.

Stefan Zweig, in his book *Mental Healers*, describes Mesmer's way of working as follows:

With a serious and dignified mien, calmly, slowly, radiating tranquility he would draw near to the patients. At his proximity a gentle fit of trembling would spread through the assembly. He wore a lilac robe, thus calling up the image of a Zoroastrian or Indian magician.

Usually no great time elapsed before one or the other of the company would begin to tremble, then the limbs would twitch convulsively, and the patient would break out in perspiration, scream or groan. No sooner had such tokens manifested themselves in one member of the chain, than the others too, would feel the onset of the famous crisis which was to bring relief. Some would fall to the ground and go into convulsions, others would laugh shrilly, others would scream, and choke, and dance like dervishes, others would appear to faint or sink into a hypnotic sleep. According to Mesmer's 'theory of crisis' the malady had to be provoked into its utmost marge of development, it had so to speak to be sweated out of the organism if the body was to remain healthy.

The importance of Mesmer to the history of coex is that, to the individuals who claim to have 'discovered' a new approach to human ills via abreaction, or say they have channelled a new cosmic force for the use of humanity, Mesmer stands as a direct contradiction. Three hundred years ago, despite his exotic dress and manner, he ran individual and group psychotherapy of a very successful nature. Although he thought of himself as a channel for a cosmic energy, he nevertheless recognised an agent other than technical psychiatric skill at work. Perhaps the 'cosmic energy' theory was not so far out either, as Reich revived it in new form in our own century. The work of Mesmer gradually moved into greater and greater complication – people dancing around trees for instance – instead of simplification and clarity. Out of it came Mesmerism which took the form of positive suggestion, completely leaving behind the aspect of allowing the organism to discharge its own tension and negativity. The spontaneous forces capable of self healing were ignored – even suppressed. The vainglorious power or forceful skill of the mesmerist or therapist took its place.

The approach started by Mesmer has never completely died out. While living in Russia in 1912 Sir Paul Dukes met Lev Lvovitch who used a self regulatory method to deal with a variety of illnesses. He would stroke patients limbs and induce shaking and trembling. In his book *Unending Quest* he describes the case of a boy whose legs were paralysed. "There was a broken exclamation from the boy in the middle of the room. 'It's b-b-beginning!' The lad was quivering from head to foot so much that he had to hold on to his chair." After several treatments Dukes observed that the boy's condition improved, and in a few weeks he was cured.

Only in very recent years has any serious scientific work been done in understanding what takes place in this healing which arises from within – with or without the help of an outside agent. Despite this research there is still virtually no socially established ways in which individuals are taught to trust their own internal processes. People in the West, and especially those trained in the helping professions, are forever committing the crime against human nature of 'doing something' to it, and seldom letting 'It' do something to them. Nevertheless some individuals and groups have done a tremendous amount to make us aware of our lack, and point out ways of overcoming it. Freud does not leave us with any sense of there being a powerful and helpful self-regulatory action in us. He gives no sense of finding a transformative power with which one can work toward spontaneous analysis and self help. But in Jung we find again and again very clear reference to what has been named in this book as coex.

Carl Jung Linking East and West

In *Psychological Commentary On The Tibetan Book of The Great Liberation*, Jung says:

> If we snatch these things directly from the East, we have merely indulged our Western acquisitiveness, confirming yet again that 'everything good is outside' whence it has to be fetched and pumped into our barren souls. It

seems to me we have really learned something from the East when we understand that the psyche contains riches enough without having to be primed from outside, and when we feel capable of evolving out of ourselves with or without divine grace... We must get at the Eastern values from within and not from without, seeking them in ourselves, in the unconscious. Because of these resistances we doubt the very thing that seems so obvious to the East, namely, the SELF LIBERATING POWER OF THE INTROVERTED MIND. This aspect of the mind is practically unknown to the West, though it forms the most important component of the unconscious.

...The whole process is called the 'transcendent function'. It is a process and a method at the same time. The production of unconscious compensation (self-regulation) is a spontaneous PROCESS; the conscious realisation is a METHOD.

In Jung we find something of the reverence for what is met within a human being – a reverence for life itself. A great deal of Jung's attitudes and thoughts have already been quoted in other chapters, enough to show that he did not use the self-regulatory process in such a cathartic way as Mesmer.

Aurobindo and Integral Yoga

During the early part of this century another great figure, in a field other than psychology, was exploring what resulted from consciousness opening to the self-regulating 'evolutionary energy'. Writing and working from the dual standpoint of an Eastern yogi and Western thinker Aurobindo explains what he found in forty years of investigating the depths and heights of inner experience. In some approaches to coex such as Pentecostalism, there is an emphasis on the transcendental, the higher potential of human nature. In other approaches the emphasis is on the cleansing or catharsis of past experience, pain and conditioning. Aurobindo finds a balance between these two which well suits the name of Integral Yoga which he gave to his system. In the book *The Adventure of Consciousness*, Satprem describes Aurobindo's statement of how the 'evolutionary force' acts on one who opens to it. "We feel around the head" he says, "and more particularly around the nape of the neck, an unusual pressure which may give the sensation of a false headache. At the beginning we can scarcely endure it for long and shake it off. Gradually this pressure takes a more distinct form and we feel a veritable current which descends – a current of force not like an unpleasant electric current but rather like a fluid mass."

To allow this spontaneously active force to work in us, Aurobindo tells us we must be quiet and open our restless mind or consciousness. In Aurobindo's own words, "When the Peace is established, this higher or Divine Force from above can descend and work in us. It descends usually first into the head and liberates inner mind centres, then into the heart centre, then into the navel and other vital centres, then into the sacral region and below. It works at the same time for perfection as well as liberation. It takes up the whole nature part by part and deals with it, rejecting what has to be rejected, sublimating what has to be sublimated, creating what has to be created. It integrates, harmonises, establishes a new rhythm in the nature. . . . The surest way toward this integral fulfilment is to find the Master of the Secret who dwells within us, open ourselves constantly to the Divine Power which is also the Divine Wisdom and Love, and trust it to effect the conversion. But it is difficult for the egoistic consciousness to do this at all at the beginning. And, if done at all, it is still difficult to do it perfectly and in every strand of our nature. It is difficult at first because of our egoistic habits of thought, of sensation, of feelings blocking up the avenues by which we arrive at the perception that is needed. It is difficult afterwards because the faith, the surrender, the courage requisite in this path are not easy to the ego clouded soul. The divine working is not the working the egoistic mind desires or approves, for it uses error to arrive at truth, suffering in order to arrive at perfection. The ego cannot see where it is being led; it revolts against the leading, loses confidence, loses courage. These failings would not matter; for the Divine Guide within is not offended by our revolt, not discouraged by our want of faith or repelled by our weakness; it has the entire love of the mother and the entire patience of the teacher. But by withdrawing our assent from the guidance we lose the consciousness, though not all the actuality of its benefit."

Reich – Cosmic Energy and the Death of Guru's

Dr. Wilhelm Reich offers us a very different approach to this world of experience. In the 1920's Reich gradually felt his way from an orthodox use of Freudian psycho-analysis to a more biological, physiological or energetic point of view. Not that he lost sight of the human soul, but he realised how much body, energy and personality are unified. By working with body attitudes or postures he found he could help the patient melt tensions and emotional blocks. By relaxing muscular tensions, flows of energy, movement and feeling were unblocked. Perhaps more than any other clinical therapist or doctor of his time, he recognised that a spontaneous, self-regulating activity or energy was at work in all living organisms. He says of this energy, which he eventually called orgone:

> Contrary to galvanic electricity – it would function on organic material which is a non-conductor for electricity, and on animal tissues. Its function would not be restricted to isloated nerve cells or cell groups, but would permeate and govern the total organism. It would have to explain in a simple way, the pulsating basic function of the living , contraction and expansion, as it is expressed in respiration and orgasm. It would express itself in the production of heat, a characteristic of most living organisms. It would definitely explain the sexual function, i.e. it would make sexual attraction understandable. It would explain what has been added to the chemically complicated protein in order to make it alive. It would, finally, have to show us the mechanism of the symmetry of form development in general.

Gradually Reich developed very definite techniques, working with respiration, muscular tension and character attitudes. He particularly explored the place of sexuality in

individual, social and political structures. He helped people
release their own self-regulatory process and work with it
toward health and wholeness. As people learnt this they
experienced spontaneous movement, trembling, changed
feeling states and emotional and sexual release. The actual
results, as compared with those already mentioned in this
short history, were no different to those in Shaktipat or in
Mesmer's work. Nevertheless Reich brought a new open-
ness, a new technical understanding to the subject with his
genius. Unlike Mesmer he did not rest until he had pin-
pointed clearly what released self-regulatory action into
conscious operation. He did not stop, as Mesmer and the
gurus did, in believing himself and certain other special
men and women were the channels of a cosmic energy
which healed. Reich made the tremendous step, while yet
remaining a scientist and clinical therapist, of seeing an
integral law of human nature at work, and active in individuals quite apart from his personal influence. In this
Reich helped people in the present to begin a link with
their spontaneous energies which earlier peoples had
known only in a religious context. The deeply religious,
surrendered attitudes so prevalent in the past are seldom
found today in the West. Certainly not in the way demonstrated by the original Christians who surrendered body
and mind to a force they trusted. Looked at in this way,
even the Godly in the West are frightened of God's power.
Jung makes the statement that people in the West cannot
find God because none of us can bow low enough. Philip
Zimbardo and Carol Laderman are more typical of the fear
we have as Westerners of the unconscious. We see in it
possible madness, loss of self, and possession by unnamed
urges and forces. Being unable to form the trust out of our
religious convictions, Reich enabled people to meet this
vital part of themselves from a different more acceptable
starting point. The new standpoint is that which includes
our critical and analytical intellect. To deny it in an attempt
to emulate the East in approaching their inner life uncriti-
cally, would be to do ourselves a great disservice. Reich
proved that as Westerners we can still touch our deep
spontaneous energies while retaining our new-found
intellect.

God's Chosen People – The Way of Subud

Considering Reich's work it is interesting now to look at the influence of Muhammed Subuh. He was born and lived in Indonesia, working as an accountant for many years. His main interest in life was to seek out some of the many gurus in his country, and attempt a deeper awareness of life's mysteries and the nature of God. In his late twenties, in the year 1925, he experienced a vision while out walking. It seemed to him that a ball of light or fire rushed across the sky and descended on his head. He began to shake and tremble, and felt a powerful and divine energy had begun to work in his being. On reaching home he opened himself to the influence of this power and found spontaneous movements and experiences occurred. From that time onwards he frequently 'opened' himself to what he felt to come from God, and found that each time movements, sounds, and a wide variety of inner experience arose. He observed that the movements and experiences were ways in which his being was gradually cleansed and made whole. It was as if some influence were gradually guiding him through experiences in a direction he could not preconceive, but IT could. Also, his physical health improved, his experiences educated him regarding his and other peoples life on Earth, and he found his intuitive faculties enormously enlarged. Often he could also be instrumental in helping other people to experience healing. The film star Eva Bartok told her story in the newspapers at the time of her own healing in connection with Pak Subuh and her baby.

By 1932 Pak Subuh had discovered that other people who relaxed in his presence could also receive the same experience and be led through cleansing and integration. Groups of people in Indonesia began to practice this 'opening' to what they felt to be the grace of God working in their lives. The manner of these group experiences is like that described under Shaktipat. People found their bodies making spontaneous movements; they experienced themselves in a wide variety of ways, were led through catharsis and great inspirational insights. Like the Pentecostal approach, there was a tendency toward remaining on the symbolic level, and editing all but the transcendental.

The experience of being moved from within was called 'Latihan', which in Indonesian means to be moved, cleansed and disciplined by the power of God. But until 1957 comparatively few people were in these groups doing latihan. Those who were had mostly been using latihan several times a week for many years. Sometimes the length of practice was ten or fifteen years. These practitioners had found that their nature and body had been gradually changed by the practice. Their awareness and sympathies had widened. Problems had shifted, and in general they felt more in touch with the force or meaning behind their existence. At this point a European working in Indonesia – Rofe – asked to be introduced to the latihan. Rofe taught it to people in England who started an international centre at Coombe Springs. From there the practice went world-wide, and at one time the followers numbers were claimed to be 200,000. People of all nationalities, religious belief, political views and social status found they could experience the latihan. The lives of many were deeply changed by it.

If we are to understand how modern men and women relate to coex there are things we must be aware of in regard to the latihan, and the organisation named Subud. J.P. Barter, for instance, writing about his involvement in the latihan says, "We do not know for any certainty why the force which is received in Subud has been made uniquely available to mankind today rather than at some earlier period in history." The statement is typical of the sort of historical blindness and spiritual pomposity that is common in the practice. Pak Subuh states that the experience is unique to him and new in the world. When I myself started a coex group many years ago, based on Reichian work and Mesmer's groups, a spy was sent from a Subud group in a nearby town to find out where or how I had stolen their latihan. That people like J.G. Bennet, a well educated man, and Barter, bright enough to write an orderly account of Subud, can accept such statements is a warning that the Western mind, in attempting to re-establish connection with the deeper layers of the psyche, can often revert to primitive attitudes, ignoring or discarding information and lessons learnt through hard experience.

Burying Old Dogmas

Another dogma in Subud, which links the organisation with the ancient guru tradition, is that no one can experience latihan without it being passed to them by someone who had received it via Pak Subuh and Subud members. It is, therefore, implied that this is not a natural occurence, or a part of everyones inner equipment, but is a special dispensation, a sort of occult power given just to Pak Subuh and members of Subud by God. The hard lessons I mentioned above are how deadly such attitudes have proved themselves to be in the past. How many millions died because sects fought each other over who had the REAL access to God and the truth? Placing the latihan in the realm of the occult and sectarian as this does, is a factor which kills its general applicability.

This revertion on the part of Westerners when meeting the unconscious is illustrated by two examples. Michael Manger visited Swami Muktananda – a Shaktipat guru – at Ganeshpuri, N.E. of Bombay. He says, "I am not sure exactly when or how I received Shaktipat as there was no formal external initiation, but it manifested itself in three ways. First an intense, wonderful and surprising tranquility of mind and body whilst sitting in the house where Babaji – the guru – was staying. Secondly, an increase in emotional and physical excitement by being in Babaji's presence and hearing him lecture. I had a pain at the base of my spine, flushed cheeks and bright eyes, despite my disagreement with the burden of Babaji's lecture – the need for a guru. Thirdly, and most important, I awoke in the middle of the night doing spontaneous breathing exercises, followed by a series of dynamic yoga postures, some known and some unknown to me. Then there were twenty minutes in which a beautiful voice emanated from my throat singing in Sanscrit – it came in verse which I wrote down and showed to Babaji the next morning.

These external happenings had two very significant internal accompaniments. Firstly an intense fire of love and light in my heart, indescribably stronger than anything I had felt previously; and secondly, direct intuitive knowledge that all this came from Babaji. It came also to a man with a communist atheist up-bringing, with but little experience of yoga or meditation and a very active belief in self help rather than guru help.

The second man, William Groom, does not make it plain whether he had planned to visit Jogeshwari to meet the guru of whether it was by chance. He says that

> ...before long a very old man appeared, and Tamhane, one of my companions presented me to him. He was Sivrao Nileshwar a Bhakti yogi who lived at Jogesh-wari, about 73 years of age and dignified in his approach. He stood in front of me with arms outstretched and took hold of my hands, the effect on me was instantaneous and electrifying. My head spun, my senses reeled, and almost immediately I became oblivious of my surroundings. Sivrao was in a deep trance from the moment he took my hands. From his throat emanated choking sounds as though he were unable to speak, whilst at the same time I could feel this powerful force flowing through his hands. This mystical experience was to become the foundation of many others which still continue with me wherever I go. I had received from the Holy Man a force or power which devotees told me is called Pare Sattva, a gift from God which they said would be with me for the rest of my life.

As can be seen from these descriptions it does not occur to these men that their experience was in any way a product of their own unconscious, despite the fact that Michael's first arose from a sleep state. The 'guru' in these cases is certainly a catalyst, helping the person to accept and trust, even believe in an inner spontaneous process. Michael's statement about his background of rational communism is almost humorous, as if communists or people with a scientific rational mind do not have an unconscious and dream life, or religious feelings. Dr. Heyer, in *Organism of the Mind*, tells of a young scientist who went for psycho-analysis because of great personal tension. As soon as he lay on the couch he burst forth in singing a hymn. By not accepting his 'irrational' nature with its religious feelings he had experienced conflict. This was resolved by allowing such feelings to be expressed.

Dianetics – Co-counselling and Accessible Coex

In the 50's Ron Hubbard published a book about his work called Dianetics. It was revolutionary in its claims of self-help psychotherapy, because until then such healing had been firmly in the hands of specialists or cults such as Subud – both being jealous of their field and requiring either high fees or membership. In a readily under-standable book Hubbard described how people could help themselves. The book gave details about re-experiencing childhood trauma, of remembering life in the womb, of full memory, and how childhood pain causes the person to function inefficiently. Unfortunately his work led to the formation of The Church of Scientology, which has signs of being another cult.

One of the offshoots of Dianetics, even though it fails to claim itself as such, is Re-Evaluation Counselling or Co-Counselling, which unlike Scientology, makes itself available to the public easily and at little or no cost. Also it clearly works with the process of self-regulation. In 1964 Harvey Jackins published a pamphlet called *The Postulates of Re-Evaluation Counselling*. In summary these postulates say that

> ...the essence of rational human behaviour consists of responding to each instant of living with a new response, created afresh at that moment to precisely fit and handle the situation of that moment as that situation is defined by the information received through the senses of the person...Each human with a physically undamaged brain has a large inherent capacity for this kind of behaviour...The natural emotional tone of a human being is zestful enjoyment of life. The natural relationship between any two human beings is loving affection, communication and cooperation. The special human capacity for rational response is interrupted by an experience of physical or emotional distress. Infor-mation input through the senses then stores as an unevaluated and rigid accumulation, exhibiting the characteristics of a very complete, literal recording of all aspects of the incident.

Immediately after the distress experience is concluded or at the first opportunity thereafter, the distressed human spontaneously seeks to claim the attention of another human. If they are successful in claiming this aware attention of the other person, a process of what has been called 'discharge' ensues.

Discharge is signalled externally by one or more of a precise set of physical processes. These are: crying or sobbing (with tears), trembling with cold perspiration, laughter, angry shouting and vigorous movement with warm perspiration, live interested talking; and in a slightly different way, yawning, often with scratching or stretching. Discharge requires considerable time for completion.

In actual practise two people contract to work together. One listens while the other talks over areas of pain or deep feeling and enters into discharge. They then swop roles. It is a very simple and effective technique. As such it cuts out all the negative aspects attendant on gurus and cults, while remaining highly effective and much more available.

The work of Dr. Caron Kent, as summarised by his book *The Puzzled Body,* while not as influential as some of the approaches mentioned, is nevertheless important. He bagan to explore coex because of his own need by giving himself regular time at a typewriter and writing spontaneously whatever came to mind. In this way he found he began to contact areas of experience and feeling previously unavailable. He developed this in his practice as a psychotherapist into working with the body and feelings directly. He writes of his work as dealing with the self-regulatory forces, and deplores physicians and therapists who are blind to their importance. One of the interesting aspects of his work is that he took careful measurements of his patients and found that as they were able to allow their being to release its own self-regulatory process, their bodies achieved their growth potential. In adults head size changed radically, as with feet, chest, etc. Kent concluded that painful or non integrated experience interfered with the growth processes in body and personality. When such experiences were released and integrated, the growth processes were released to complete their work.

Ronnie Laing Daring to Care

Someone who has had a very widespread and revolutionary influence on psychiatric and non-clinical therapy is R.D. Laing. His book *The Politics of Experience*, published in 1967, sums up his view of how the sane and the so-called insane can be helped by forming a supportive environment in which self-regulation can take place. He says in the book:

> No age in the history of humanity has perhaps so lost touch with this natural 'healing' process, that implicates some of the people whom we label schizophrenic. No age has so developed it, no age had imposed such prohibitions and deterrences against it, as our own. Instead of the mental hospital, which is a sort of re-servicing factory for human breakdowns, we need a place where people who have travelled further and, consequently, may be more lost than psychiatrists and other sane people, can find their way 'further' into inner space and time, and back again. Instead of the 'degradation' ceremonial of psychiatric examination, diagnosis and prognostication, we need, for those who are ready for it, an initiation ceremonial, through which the person will be guided with full social encouragement and sanction, into inner space and time, by people who have been there and back again. Psychiatrically this would appear as ex-patients helping future patients to go mad.
>
> What is entailed then is:
>
>   **i** A voyage from outer to inner,
>   **ii** from life to a kind of death,
> **iii** from going forward to going back,
>   **iv** from temporal movement to temporal standstill,
>   **v** from mundane time to aeonic time,
>   **vi** from the ego to the self,
> **vii** from being outside (post birth) back into the womb of all things (pre birth).
>
> And then subsequently a return voyage from:
>
> **1** Inner to outer,
> **2** from death to life,
> **3** from the movement back to a movement forward,

4 from immortality back to mortality,
5 from eternity back to time,
6 from self to a new ego,
7 from a cosmic foetalisation to an existential rebirth.

...This process may be one that all of us need, in one form or another. The process could have a central function in a truly sane society.

The Japanese Have Seitai

While teaching coex in Japan I was introduced to another Oriental approach to self-regulation which is widely used in that country. It is called Seitai and was taught in its present form by Haruchika Noguchi. In Japan Seitai is thought of as a way of keeping healthy, but it has a particular quality about it which comes out in Noguchi's teachings. He constantly stressed that you cannot understand what a human being is by dissecting one, or by trying to understand the function of separate organs such as the liver or brain.

For instance, he said that,

One person may find his appetite increases when he is in love, another may find that his heart rather than his stomach responds. Similarly, the same stressful situation may result in rheumatism in one person and diabetes in another. What causes these differences? Some individuals are so tough they are calm even with a million pound debt, while others become ill over obligations of only ten pounds. The physical tendencies of each person are different, and unless one takes ones stand on this fact the health problems of different people cannot be grasped.

Seitai's starting point is from a completely different concept of health to that of a keep-fit class. In keep-fit, and in just about every form of exercise from yoga to weight training, there are certain movements or postures which are said to exercise particular muscles, or to be 'good' for the thighs, abdomen, etc. These are then applied or practised from outside, as it were. Seitai has the concept that our life process knows what sort, and how much exercise we need, and the exercise arises from within. In other words it is stimulated by our unconscious sense of our own needs, just as a sneeze is.

Let me quote Noguchi again to explain this. He says,

> In my teens I started to guide people to health by means of what we now call Seitai Soho and Katsugen Undo, though at that time I had no knowledge of medicine or of the body's anatomical structure. I did not know anything about the kind of food we should eat, yet I was able to lead people to health.
>
> What was the basis for the guidance? It was that I asked myself why human beings stayed alive and what should be done to activate their strength to live... We find various excuses for suppressing ourselves and, without realising we are putting our innate powers for health asleep, we convince ourselves that we are weak and blame it on our surroundings, the food we eat or the hours we sleep, unaware that the real responsibility lies with us.

So Seitai creates a situation in which we listen and allow response. Noguchi taught that the spontaneous movements which arise as the response are the same as those occurring during sleep. Seitai considers whether our vitality and enthusiasm for life is active or withdrawn. If withdrawn, then it is encouraged to express itself again. Because a great deal of the suppressive factors in us are mental and emotional, Seitai encourages a strong and healthy confidence in ones ability to survive. If we fear we will become ill if a night's sleep is missed, the anxiety creates tension which suppresses the defence systems of the body. If illness then occurred, would it mean one was naturally sickly?

Put in another way, we are learning to allow the body's own natural mechanisms, such as the eyes watering if dust enters them, and other such more subtle reactions, to function more vitally. Noguchi stresses that it is not the movements of Seitai which heal us. The symptoms of illness are the body's own attempts to heal itself, and Seitai helps us work with that process. To do the movements mechanically as if they were the thing which healed, is to miss the point and would be a return to keep-fit. But once you have learnt to allow your body to heal itself more vigorously, you do not need to practise it any more.

Coming right up to the present, Rolfing, Primal Therapy, EST, Re-Birthing, Bioenergetics, all offer their particular genius to a culture convulsing with activity to become whole. Unfortunately most of these approaches offer their help through highly paid experts to those who feel in need of paying for it. The Expert/Patient relationship is something which is badly in need of renovation. As Laing suggests, what we need is not more experts and organisations, but something seen as a central function in a sane society. We need courage and faith in our own ability to move toward wholeness – and companions who will be with us while we experience the journey.

The Work of Herman Weiner

One of the problems with the development of self determinism in therapy is the changed social and financial situation of the therapists themselves. In an article called 'Working With Groups' Herman Weiner says:

> As a psychoanalytically trained therapist, I conducted analytically oriented groups for several years during the sixties and I duly had my share of 'success'. Try as I might to be open and free-feeling, I would end up at some point in the group process somewhat more guarded. I also observed that this pulling back was periodically reached by my patients...It became difficult to feel less neurotic than my patients seemed to be. A very humbling experience! I ultimately decided to give up groups and to work on a one-to-one basis.

Returning to group work later he organised a different group dynamics, which he describes as the

> patients enter a semi-darkened well padded, sound dampened set of adjoining rooms...They already know what to do for themselves from an initial series of individual preparatory sessions. They are beginning to know that courage to let themselves sense, move, fantasise and feel without restraint, is both liberating and

healing. In the initial sessions they have been encouraged to surrender themselves to themselves in this manner. Now, in the semi-darkness, I move from one mat to another giving support, courage, and contact where necessary, so as to facilitate their descent into themselves.

Without the historical background to Herman Weiner's work, we would not realise that he is doing nothing new. In fact he is still attempting to play the central role for his 'patients'. Even Subud gives more autonomy, and Co-Counselling exhibits the deep trust of help in healing to whoever can give 'aware attention'.

Love is the Key to Changing Lives

While Janov's work has reminded the world of the need to discharge pain and anger, from our consideration of coex it does not have a great deal to say. With Bioenergetics also, though Lowen's writings are full of self-regulatory principles, based as they are on Reich's work, it is still a therapist/patient oriented technique.

Something which enters more deeply into general social applicability is the work being done by Jacques Schiff in U.S.A. A person of obviously great love and wisdom, she and her husband adopted several teenage 'children' and allowed them full opportunity to self-regulate right in their home. These children were often the apparently hopeless cases from mental hospitals, and were allowed to regress to being in nappies again, bottle feeding, and to work through their stages of growth in a healthier way than had originally occurred. As she shows clearly in her book – *All My Children* – the self-regulatory release these young adults had was only half what was needed in their healing. The other half, as Jackins points out, comes through consciously re-evaluating the experience released in coex.

Once she had brought several of her 'children' through to health, although she and her husband are psychiatrists, she encouraged other families to use the same methods. Some of the 'children' now adult, have set up their own fostering family setting. These new family groups are likewise raising healthy children out of sick adults.

LSD and the 'Heavy' Drug Scene

Because of the struggle our culture is having with drug abuse, it is necessary here to point out that a few of the 'drugs', notably psilocybin, LSD and Cannabis, all release self-regulatory experience. However, if the person does not integrate what is released by the drug, marked disorientation occurs. What have been called 'flash backs' are exactly the same as what is described by William Groom after meeting his guru – "still continue with me wherever I go." In his case he wanted these inner eruptions of experience. If a person were frightened of the unconscious, as Philip Zimbardo describes, the 'flash backs' can be very disturbing.

Some of the most effective work with the principle of coex was done with LSD prior to its banishment. A number of psychiatrists were registered to work with it. To understand this positive side to these drugs, it is useful to read such books as *Myself and I* by Constance Newland; and *LSD Psychotherapy* by W.V. Caldwell. When compared with the literature on 'tripping', the tremendous difference can be seen between playing with and working with, the inner process of coex.

Summary

In the widest sense self-regulation is an integral part of all human experience. It is particularly noticeable historically in the religions of humanity. The ball of fire Pak Subuh mentions has been described by many other religious leaders. It appeared to the disciples at Pentecost. When we realise that the dream process in the coex experience produces just such waking subjective impressions, it becomes obvious that a similar and universal psychobiological process underlies such human activities.

In different ages humans have met with, used and directed the self-regulatory process in different ways. We have given the experience of consciously working with such processes the name coex, and in the past it has been given many names and many explanations. The physical and subjective experiences which occur in coex, because of their connection with the dream process, frequently produce a sense of touching the divine. This is the way our internal interpretative process expresses contact between our conscious personality and the universal life forces which give rise to it. Unfortunately, groups gathered around leaders who give their experience of coex different names such as Christianity, Buddhism, Subud and Mesmerism, frequently argue for their own uniqueness. In most cases however, as with Christianity, the original direct experience is quickly suppressed.

The historical perspective shows us not only how people lay claim to ownership of a natural principle, but also how they have a tendency to limit it to their own horizons and belief systems. Even Reich was guilty of claiming himself as the first man in history to use the process. But few have, indeed, dared to spell out its political and social implications as clearly as he. The released inner response of our being is revolutionary in nature. This is probably why established traditions of religion, medicine and politics often suppress any signs of its appearance. There is a lesson to be learned from Mesmer's clash with his fellow physicians. As hundreds received relief from pain, thousands more came. This led Mesmer to 'magnetise' anything that was handy, such as a tree, so people would be free of his counselling rooms. His popularity and excess led the French Academy of Science to set up a commission to examine Mesmer's claims. They concluded that "Nothing proves the existence of magnetic animal fluid: imagination without magnetism may produce conversions: magnetism without imagination produces nothing." While that may be true, Mesmer was discredited, and none of his critics managed to mobilise peoples 'imagination' sufficiently to cure the ills of the public in his place...Reich died in a prison cell.